RAND LABOR AND POPULATION

Inequality and Opportunity

The Relationship Between Income Inequality and Intergenerational Transmission of Income

Francisco Perez-Arce, Ernesto F. L. Amaral, Haijing Huang, Carter C. Price

For more information on this publication, visit www.rand.org/t/RR1509

Library of Congress Cataloging-in-Publication Data
ISBN: 978-0-8330-9488-9

Published by the RAND Corporation, Santa Monica, Calif.

Cover: EVGENY KOVALEV/Fotolia.

Preface

Income inequality has been increasing in developed countries, as earnings at the bottom of the income scale have stagnated and the incomes of educated workers and top earners have risen. Some fear that income inequality will curtail outcomes for poor children by giving them less opportunity to climb the economic ladder.

Several policies have been proposed to alleviate inequality. Of these, some aim to directly reduce inequality in outcomes by, for example, providing cash transfers to the poor to reduce income disparities. Other policies directly target inequality in opportunities, such as those that provide financial aid to college students or early childhood education. However, inequality in opportunities and inequality in outcomes are interrelated, and both sets of policies are likely to have effects on opportunities and outcomes. They deserve to be studied together.

The aim of this report is to help the reader better understand the relationship between inequality in outcomes and inequality in opportunity, defined as the degree to which conditions at birth and childhood determine outcomes later in life. A deeper understanding of the relationship can lead to a better appraisal of policies that could provide greater opportunities for all.

Funding for this study was provided by philanthropic contributions from RAND supporters and income from operations. This research was undertaken within RAND Labor and Population. RAND Labor and Population has built an international reputation for conducting objective, high-quality, empirical research to support and improve policies and organizations around the world. Its work focuses on children and families, demographic behavior, education and training, labor markets, social welfare policy, immigration, international development, financial decisionmaking, and issues related to aging and retirement with a common aim of understanding how policy and social and economic forces affect individual decisionmaking and human well-being.

For more information on RAND Labor and Population, contact

Unit Director
RAND Labor and Population
1776 Main Street, P.O. Box 2138
Santa Monica, CA 90407-2138
(310) 393-0411

or visit the Labor and Population homepage at http://www.rand.org/labor.

Contents

Figures

Tables

Summary

In the United States and most other developed countries, income inequality has been growing, regardless of whether income is measured at the household or individual level; this finding holds for a variety of data sources and measures of inequality. The significant increase in income inequality in developed countries has been driven mostly by a combination of increased wages for highly educated workers and higher incomes for top earners (often managers of large companies and a few other high-paying occupations), and a stagnation of incomes in the middle of the distribution. A large fraction of the increases in income inequality is explained by the divergence of incomes between those in the top 1 percent and the rest. Public programs have allowed poverty to decline even amid general increases in inequality.

In this report, we analyze the likely impacts of these changes on inequality of opportunity. The higher incomes of highly skilled workers might allow them to invest more in their children, which could lead to greater inequality of investment in children's skills. However, the most important factor in the recent increase in inequality—higher incomes at the top of the income distribution—would affect inequality in opportunity among only a fraction of the population. In addition, increased public support for the poor may have limited the impact of increased income and wealth inequality on inequality in opportunity.

There is empirical evidence regarding the extent to which economic inequality and inequality of opportunity move together across time and geographies. The results of a meta-regression analysis designed to answer this particular question (Amaral and Perez-Arce, 2015) show that, across countries, there is a correlation between income inequality and proxy measures of inequality of opportunity. However, across time *within a country*, increases in inequality are not always accompanied by increases in inequality of opportunity. Overall, the strong cross-country correlation, but weak or null within-country, cross-time correlation, suggests that there is no unequivocal connection between the two types of inequality. Thus, a closer examination of the different links between inequality of opportunity and inequality of outcomes is warranted.

An analysis of how parents' income relates to their children's income, which can drive the relationship between inequality and inequality of opportunity, shows that capital is transferred directly—primarily through gifts and inheritance. This yields a correlation in capital income between parents and their children. But, more important, intergenerational labor income is also correlated, which comes about through the transfer of skills, genetic and environmental factors, and investments in education and child development. The evidence regarding the relative importance of each of these linkages makes it clear that investing in children's skills (through direct or indirect investments, such as the choice of school and time spent rearing children) is a major driver of the correlation.

This evidence can illustrate the policies that can reduce inequality of opportunity and inequality of outcomes. We use the framework to analyze how the incomes of children are linked to those of their parents and what can affect those linkages. To demonstrate the magnitude of the potential effect of policies, we use estimates from previous research to conduct simple simulations that demonstrate how a modeling exercise can be used to study the impact of policies on the inequality of opportunity. We discuss how full simulation models could be built to provide accurate predictions of the impact of different policies on inequality of outcomes and opportunity.

Acknowledgments

This work was conducted as part of the RAND-Initiated Research program and was funded by the generosity of RAND's donors and by fees earned on client funded research.

We are grateful to Lynn S. Karoly, Krishna Kumar, Shanthi Nataraj, and Richard Neu for generous and constructive feedback. Special thanks to Melissa Bauman and Rebecca Fowler, whose review greatly improved the presentation of this report. We also thank Samantha Bennett for editing the report, Beth Bernstein for managing the document production, and Tanya Maiboroda for designing the cover.

The RAND Labor and Population review process employs anonymous peer reviewers, including at least one reviewer who is external to RAND. We benefited from the thorough and constructive feedback provided by two anonymous reviewers.

Abbreviations

AFDC	Aid to Families with Dependent Children
CBO	Congressional Budget Office
EITC	earned income tax credit
GDP	gross domestic product
GGC	Great Gatsby Curve
IGE	intergenerational income elasticity
IGTI	intergenerational transmission of income
MTO	Movement to Opportunity
OECD	Organisation for Economic Co-operation and Development
SBTC	skill-biased technological change
TANF	Temporary Assistance to Needy Families
WTID	World Top Income Database

CHAPTER ONE

Introduction

The United States, like much of the developed world, has seen a rise in the primary measures of income inequality over the last four decades. These trends have been driven largely by rapid increases in the concentration at top of the income distribution. Beyond concerns about inequality in and of itself, some economists and commentators have expressed various concerns about the negative implications of this trend. Some worry about the potential impact of inequality on economic growth.[1] Others are concerned that income inequality harms democratic representativeness. While these are important areas of study, this report focuses on the impact that inequality of outcomes (e.g., income inequality or wealth) has on inequality of opportunity, understood as the extent to which conditions at birth and childhood determine adult outcomes.

Inequality in outcomes and inequality in opportunities may be related through several channels. For example, inequality in parental income translates into disparities in the investments parents can make in their children, thereby affecting inequality in opportunities. Furthermore, larger disparities in the opportunities that children have can translate into inequality in their outcomes in their adult lives.

We aim to understand the extent to which inequalities in outcomes (such as earnings, income, and wealth) are related to inequality in opportunities for subsequent generations, as well as which mechanisms drive their relationship. A deeper understanding of that relationship can then lead us to a better appraisal of the potential of policies to "level the playing field." A large number of public policies intend to tackle either inequality of outcomes or inequality of opportunity. We find that policies targeting inequality in income at a given point in time are likely to affect the opportunity of newer generations. Similarly, policies aimed at increasing opportunity and intergenerational mobility are likely to affect income inequality, as measured in a single point in time. Thus, assessment of policies should account for their likely impact on both income inequality and inequality of opportunity.

The rest of this report is organized into five chapters. In Chapter Two, we develop a simple framework to understand the relationship between income inequality and inequality of opportunity. We introduce the concepts of inequality of opportunity and inequality in outcomes, as well as the measures we use to track them.

In Chapter Three, we summarize the most-important recent trends in inequality of outcomes (income and wealth). We briefly discuss the driving forces behind them, and their likely

[1] The economic literature has not reached consensus about whether inequality adversely affects economic growth, though recent high-profile studies have found evidence that locations with higher levels of inequality, at a specific point in time, have lower future economic growth than places with lower inequality.

impacts on inequality of opportunity according to the framework in Chapter Two. We find that income inequality has been growing, regardless of whether income is measured at the household or individual level, and that this finding is robust to the data source and the measure of inequality used. Several factors are likely contributing to the growth of income inequality. The wages of highly educated workers have grown more than those of the less educated. Some of this growth is fueled by changes in technology and higher incomes for top earners (often managers of large companies), due in part to globalization and information technology permitting managers to control larger operations. At the bottom of the distribution, wages have been affected by institutional changes, such as the real-term decrease in minimum wages, the weaker role of trade unions, and increased international trade. However, public programs and higher female labor force participation have moderated the impact of these factors on poverty. One could expect that higher incomes of skilled workers might translate into greater investments in their children and thus higher inequality of investment in children's skills. However, available measures of the intergenerational transmission of income, which we use as a proxy for inequality of opportunity, do not show a similarly clear upward trend.

Chapter Four analyzes the relationship between inequality of outcomes and inequality of opportunity. We first present empirical evidence regarding the extent to which income inequality and proxies for inequality of opportunity move together across time and geographies. We show that, across countries, there is a robust correlation between income inequality and the proxy measures for inequality of opportunity. However, across time, increases in income inequality are not always accompanied by increases in inequality of opportunity. This suggests that the drivers of cross-country differences in income inequality are different from those that drive differences within a country and across time.

The second part of this chapter describes the different links through which the incomes of children and parents are related, as well as which links may drive a relationship between inequality of income and inequality of opportunity. Capital is transferred directly—primarily through gifts and inheritance—which yields a correlation in capital income. But, more important, intergenerational labor income is also correlated through the transfer of skills, which occurs through several channels—e.g., genetic and environmental factors and investments in education and child health. There is evidence of causal links between parental education and income and the human capital of their children, which suggests that policy can reduce inequality in opportunity by increasing the economic opportunities for children of low-income families.

Our ultimate objective is to use this evidence to illustrate how policies can affect these interrelated concepts of inequality. For example, an income transfer to the poor reduces contemporaneous income inequality but may also reduce inequality of opportunity if the transfers affect the investments that poorer families make in their children. If so, the income transfer may also change future income inequality because it would change the distribution of skills. In Chapter Five we gauge which policies can have an impact on inequality of opportunity and inequality of outcomes. To demonstrate the magnitude of the potential effect of policies, we use estimates from previous research to conduct simple simulations that illustrate how a modeling exercise can be carried out to study the impact of policies on the inequality of opportunity.

Chapter Six presents our conclusions and lays the groundwork for further research.

CHAPTER TWO

Framework for Understanding Inequality in Income and Opportunity

This chapter presents a simple framework of income and opportunity inequality and discusses different measures and proxies of these concepts. We argue that, depending on the sources of the increase in inequality, we may expect different consequences for inequality of opportunity.

Concepts and Measures of Inequality and Inequality in Opportunity

Throughout this report, we focus on two broad concepts of inequality. The first, and most common in the economic literature, is *inequality of outcomes*, which refers to the extent to which there is variation in outcomes, such as income and wealth in a population. This may refer to variation in the amounts that people earn (*income inequality*) or what people have (*wealth inequality*).[1] While this may seem notionally straightforward, there are a variety of ways to define both income and wealth, and there are also several ways to measure inequality. While there may be reasons to prefer one measure to another for specific questions, together the various metrics can provide a textured view of the economic landscape and how it has changed over time.

Income can be measured in a variety of ways, including annually or over a lifetime, for individuals or households, and as either market or disposable income. *Market income* refers to the income earned directly from labor (*earned income* or *earnings*) and capital (*capital income*), while *disposable income* subtracts taxes paid and adds public transfers received. Thus, market income provides a starting point for looking at income inequality, and the comparison with disposable income can help assess the impact of some government programs and policies. Neither type of income presents a complete picture, but together they can paint a more detailed picture.

Likewise, there are a host of inequality measures that can be used to provide a nuanced understanding of the distribution in question. While simple statistical measures, such as the standard deviation, are frequently used to understand distributions, they are less useful for understanding changes in inequality over time because they can be affected by inflation. Thus, economists have preferred measures that do not depend on the mean of the distribution—i.e., measures that are unchanged if the whole distribution is shifted or multiplied by an integer. The measure most commonly published by statistical agencies is the Gini coefficient, which can be interpreted as a function of the mean difference. (For example, if we take any two U.S.

[1] For many purposes, we would like to measure inequality as the variation in earning capacity—in other words, some individuals earn less because they choose occupations that have more desirable characteristics but pay less (called compensating wage differentials).

households at random, the expected difference is two times the Gini coefficient's percentage of the mean; see Atkinson and Morelli, 2014.) Since the Gini coefficient is a function of the mean difference, any change in the relative income, either at the bottom or the top of the distribution, will affect measured inequality. The Gini coefficient reduces the level of inequality into a single number, but this simplicity omits much of the texture and context of some other approaches to measuring inequality.

Another class of inequality measures—the "shape measures"—is based on specific parts of the distribution, such as the top, middle, and bottom. Percentile comparisons provide ways of looking at the shape of the distribution. Poverty measures, while not directly metrics of inequality, capture the deprivation at the bottom of the distribution. Likewise, the share of income going to the top is frequently used to assess inequality trends driven by concentration among high earners. It is an important measure because (as we describe in Chapter Five) much of the recent increases in inequality have been driven by higher incomes among the top 1 percent. However, this measure is unaffected by changes in the shape of the middle and bottom of the distribution and thus tells only part of the story.

Inequality of opportunity is a less concrete notion, related to the degree to which everyone has the same opportunities to achieve outcomes. Conceptually, inequality of opportunity can be thought of as the extent to which conditions at birth (including socioeconomic status of the parents) affect the likelihood of a specific economic outcome as an adult (Roemer et al., 2003). While it is not possible to assess inequality of opportunity directly, realized opportunity can be measured using *intergenerational transmission of income* (IGTI), or *intergenerational mobility* (we use these terms interchangeably). IGTI refers to how much of adults' income of is determined by the income of their parents while they were raising children; IGTI thereby attempts to capture inequality of opportunity. In practice, IGTI can be approximated by measuring the differences in the probability that children from different socioeconomic backgrounds reach different relative positions in the income distribution when adults. Alternatively, we can use measures that capture the proportional difference in earnings of those born to wealthier versus poorer parents.

There are two sets of proxy measures for IGTI. The first set is measures based on how a person's position in the income distribution is related to that of his or her parents. We refer to them as *relative measures* of intergenerational mobility. A common measure is the probability that an adult's earnings will be in the top quintile, conditional on being born to a family whose earnings were in the bottom quintile. Studies sometimes compute the full "transition matrix" of children's versus parents' quintile positions. A second measure within this set consists of simply estimating the *parental income correlation*: the correlation between child and parental earnings. A more complete but less commonly used measure consists of dividing earnings into multiple centiles and then estimating using a regression model where the dependent (right-hand side) variable is the centile position of the parent and the independent (left-hand side) variable is the position of the child (we refer to this measure as the *rank-rank correlation*).

The second set of proxy measures looks at how the *level* of earnings of the children and the parents are related. We refer to these as *elasticity measures of intergenerational mobility*. One can estimate the elasticity of children's earnings to that of their parents—that is, the predicted percentage change of a child's earning based on a percentage change in his or her parent's earnings. (For example, in the United States, a child born to a parent whose earnings were 10 percent higher than the mean will earn on average 5 percent more than the mean.) This elasticity, termed *intergenerational elasticity* (IGE), is usually estimated through a regression of the logarithm of a measure of the child's earnings against the logarithm of the parent's earnings. The IGE measure is a function of the parent-child correlation, described above, but also of the variance of income in the parent's and child's generations.[2]

Measures based on the position within the distribution (such as the rank-rank correlation) are unrelated to current dispersion in wages; these measures simply aim to capture how much a father's position on the income ladder matters to the position of the offspring.[3] In contrast, IGE is directly affected by dispersion of earnings in the child's generation, which can drive the relationship between inequality and inequality of opportunity in a mechanical way. The same rank-rank correlation will translate into a higher IGE when the income distribution in the child's generation is wide and a lower IGE when income is more tightly distributed. Thus, even without changes in the relative measures of income mobility, an increase in income inequality would translate into higher-elasticity measures of intergenerational mobility. The IGE is important as well because it tells us how much the position of parents "matters."

It should be noted that these mobility measures tend to be applied to income and not wealth. This is partly because of data limitations involving the scarcity of accurate and complete wealth data relative to income data, which makes it challenging to empirically produce comparable estimates for wealth mobility.

Income Generation and Sources of Income Disparities

Now that we have established the outcomes of interest, the concepts of opportunity, and some ways of measuring them, we present a framework for investigating their relationship. The simple framework below sets the stage for much of the discussion that follows. Essentially, we are seeking to understand how inequality in one generation will pass on to future generations through an inequality of opportunities.

For this framework, the important actors to consider are individuals and households. Households are composed of a number of individuals who generate income through the use of their capital—either physical or human—in the market. Each individual has a certain level of skills (human capital), decides whether to work and how much (the intensity of use), and earns an income (the return to the asset), depending on the market wage for his or her skills. Similarly, individuals invest their (physical) capital and earn income depending on the rate of return (such as the interest rate).[4] The first equation in Figure 2.1 provides a visual representation of this idea.

---

[2] IGE equals the child-parent correlation multiplied by the ratio of the standard deviation of the log of child income to the standard deviation of the log of parent income.

[3] Frequently, the father's income is used for these estimations to avoid complications with fairly measuring women's income, because of changes in workforce participation related to childbirth. Similarly, some studies focus on father-son income relationships. Given rising labor force participation rates among women, this segregation may not be necessary in the future.

[4] Figure 2.1 provides a simple representation, though a more precise representation of this income-generation process would be given by $I_{t,g}(HC,C,A)=W_{t,g}(HC,A,h,a)+R_{t,g}(C,Ic,A,a)$. Market income is a sum of labor income and capital income. Labor income is expressed as a time- and place-dependent wage function, which largely depends on the skills possessed (*HC* = human capital) and intensity of use, namely time and effort spent working (*h* = hours worked). Potentially, other assets (*A*) used with intensity (such as social connections) may affect how skills and effort are combined to generate labor earnings.

Figure 2.1
Market and Disposable Income in the Simple Framework

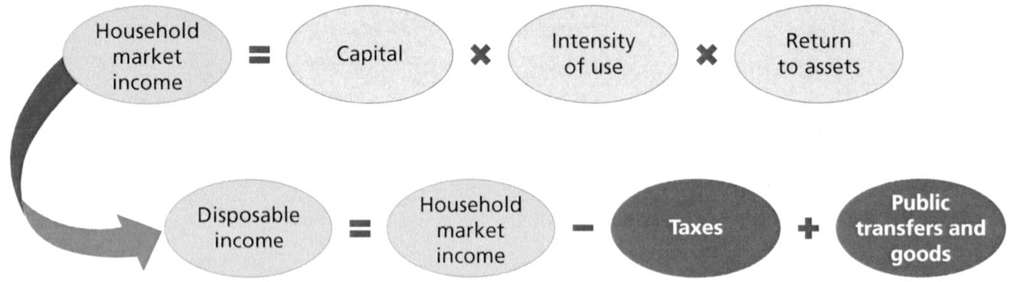

RAND *RR1509-2.1*

From market income, households pay taxes, and some receive cash transfers from the government, such as welfare payments, subsidies, or social security, leaving them with *disposable income* to pay for goods and services (the second equation of Figure 2.1).[5]

Market income inequality arises through

1. differences in the amount and type of *capital* owned: These disparities are partly a result of inheritance but also of past behavior (decisions regarding how much to save or how much to invest in human capital—for example, by obtaining more schooling)
2. differences in the *intensity of use* of capital: Intensity of the use of skill (labor) takes form in the decisions of whether or not to work, how much to work, and how hard
3. the *returns* that individuals receive: Different types of assets (for example, a stock versus bond or high-school education versus college education) will typically fetch different returns. In a market economy, identical assets would earn the same return, though there could be geographical disparities. For instance, wages for similar work and skill level in a large city may be higher than in a rural community, which contributes to differences in returns and market earnings. Furthermore, over time, inequality may widen if returns to certain assets—typically under the purview of high-income families, such as higher levels of education—increase.

Disposable income inequality—the income that individuals have available for consumption and investment—can differ substantially from market income, both in absolute terms and relative to others', due to taxes and to transfers from the public sector. In fact, as we discuss later, much of the cross-country variation in income inequality arises from the role of the public sector. Progressive taxes reduce inequality but may also reduce incentives to work or invest, which can create inefficiencies and a potential decrease in aggregate income.

The wage function (*Wt,g*) is time and place dependent, so the return to skills is different across time and space. Similarly, capital (*C*) produces a return (*R*), depending on how much of it is invested and where (*Ic*).

[5] Note, however, that the equations do not assume that assets, the intensity of use, and the return enter the equation multiplicatively, as could be interpreted from the figure.

Inequality of Opportunity and the Intergenerational Transmission of Income

As will be discussed in Chapter Four, the earnings of parents and their children are empirically correlated. This fact could be explained with several plausible linkages within the framework above. These linkages will be useful when assessing the potential mechanisms through which income inequality can affect inequality of opportunity. As Figure 2.2 shows, a direct connection may exist between income of parents and their children. More income allows families to invest in their children through better nutrition, enrichment activities, university fees, and so on. In Chapter Five, we present the evidence about the causal link of income and children's human capital.

An important channel for intergenerational transmission is the transmission of parents' capital to their children (Figure 2.3). The most obvious transmission is through gifts and

Figure 2.2
Types of Assets and the Human Capital Formation Process

Capital	Intensity of use	Return	How is it built?
Capital	**Invested (stock market, housing) or "under the bed"**	**Interest rate, etc.**	**Savings**
Skills: Cognitive and noncognitive skills/education Labor market experience	Labor market participation	Wages for different types of employment/skills Returns to schooling	Early childhood education Health Labor market participation
Other: Social capital, (social connections)	Use of social connections in economic activity	Wage premiums in certain jobs/unions	

RAND *RR1509-2.2*

Figure 2.3
Links Between Income of Parents and Children

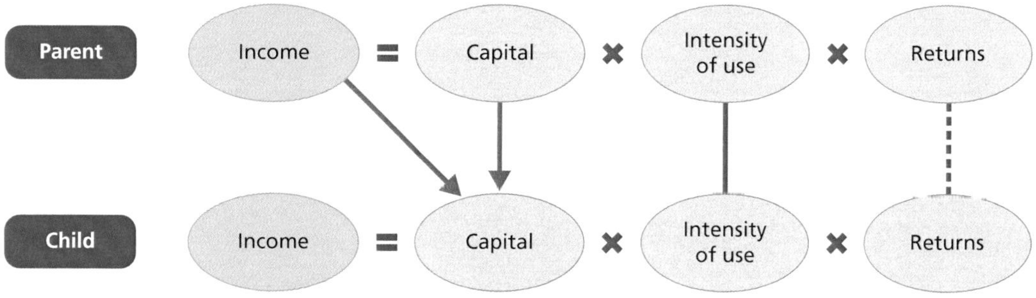

NOTE: Arrows denote causal effects. Solid line denotes correlation. Dashed line presents correlation at certain level of locality (i.e., correlation due to tendency of children to live in the same locality or state as their parents).
RAND *RR1509-2.3*

inheritances, but skills also can be transmitted from parents to children (we present a brief overview on the literature on human capital formation in Chapter Five). Parental income and wealth could also be transmitted to their children through high skills if they are used to buy access to better schooling (for example, through housing in high-performing school districts) or other experiences that affect human capital accumulation.

The returns to different types of capital may also correlate to the extent that children live in the same areas as their parents. There are frictions (transaction costs of moving, location-specific social capital, and preferences) that result in children tending to live close to where they grew up. Thus, if geographical differences in returns to assets are persistent, there is a correlation between the returns faced by parents and children living in proximity.

These linkages can explain why income inequality may be correlated with inequality of opportunity. Different drivers of income and wealth inequality would affect inequality of opportunity differently. For instance, an increase in the concentration of wealth (changes in the distribution of *assets* according to the framework above) would likely make society less financially mobile (less equality of opportunity), since wealth can be easily transmitted across generations. On the other hand, increased inequality through higher returns to skill or education may not have such a large effect (a larger differential of the payoff to education might increase the differences in earnings but might not reduce the probability that a child achieves a given level of education or earnings), except through the increased opportunities for investment in their children's assets.[6]

[6] However, increased inequality through higher returns to skill or education may have an indirect effect, since those earning a higher return may be able to use that income to invest in their children. We discuss the possible linkages more fully in Chapter Five and the evidence regarding the importance of each of these linkages.

CHAPTER THREE

Trends in Inequality

In this chapter, we first take a brief look at longer-run trends in income inequality before delving into a more in-depth analysis of the recent trends. After describing the trends in household and individual income inequality since the 1980s, we discuss what these trends could imply for inequality of opportunity. The discussion refers to the U.S. case, but we present some comparisons to other developed countries as well.

Long-Run Trends in Inequality

In broad (and perhaps overly simplistic) terms, reductions in inequality during the most of the 20th century were marked by increases in the *levels* of accumulation of assets—most notably education and skills—by large swaths of the population. That is to say, inequality fell during these periods because income and wealth at the middle and bottom of the distribution increased substantially in both absolute and relative terms. In contrast, increases in inequality since the 1980s have been driven mostly by a change in *returns to those assets*, particularly the returns to education and skill. We discuss the likely causes of the changes in returns in Appendix A.

Kuznets (1955) hypothesized that inequality would first rise and then decline as a country developed; this is commonly known as the Kuznets inverted-U curve. Our simple framework can illustrate Kuznets' hypothesis. Individuals possess capital, which can be employed to produce a return (for example, investing capital in the stock market, or using skills to earn wages). In a very primitive society, production depends mostly on unsophisticated labor. Increases in productivity create the opportunity for asset accumulation, which in turn creates the opportunity for inequality. The first individuals who accumulate assets drive inequality up. In Kuznets' original exposition, the economic shift from agriculture to industry drove such an increase in inequality. Once the majority of people have moved from agriculture to higher-paid employment in industry, additional movers to industry result in reduced inequality.

Up until the 1980s, Kuznets' prediction about the relationship between growth and inequality held up fairly well for the United States and many other (now-developed) countries. Historical investigations show inequality being relatively low in preindustrial societies (Milanovic, Lindert, and Williamson, 2007) and increasing as countries industrialized. Meanwhile, Atkinson, Piketty, and Saez (2011) and Piketty (2014) show a decrease in the income shares going to top percentiles of earners (particularly the top 1 percent but also the top 5 percent) during the early-to-mid 20th century.[1]

During the late 18th and 19th centuries, while the United States was industrializing, inequality increased steadily (Lindert and Williamson, 2012). Inequality reached its peak at the turn of the 20th century and started decreasing after that, amid further industrialization and growth. Countries that started industrializing later saw their inequality rising later, and it started declining later as well (for example, Brandolini and Vecchi, 2011, compare the historical patterns for Italy and Spain).

In the United States, during most of the 20th century, educational opportunities expanded throughout the population, contributing to further growth and less inequality (Goldin and Katz, 2010). Though there are no estimates of the trends in intergenerational transmission of income measures, or other proxy measures for equality of opportunity, it is important to note that growth and reductions of inequality were strongly affected by the accumulation of human capital by the broader population. The share of families with at least one college graduate grew substantially during the postwar period (Goldin and Katz, 2001 and 2010). Because of the relationship between education and income, this trend suggests that inequality of opportunity was decreasing concurrently with inequality of income. The same pattern can be seen in most developed countries, with those that developed earlier reaching their inequality peak earlier.[2]

Inequality in the United States and most other developed nations has risen significantly since the 1980s. Panel B of Figure 3.1 shows how inequality in developed nations started to climb in the 1980s, while gross domestic product (GDP) per capita continued to rise (Panel A).[3] Though the rise in inequality since the 1980s in the United States has been one of the steepest, it is not the only country experiencing this phenomenon. The next sections contain a discussion of the trends in the income distribution since 1980 and the implications these trends have had on opportunity. We then discuss trends in the proxy measures of inequality of opportunity over this period.

[1] This was marked in particular by a reduction of capital income (and the share of capital income from total income), as well as a deconcentration of capital and wealth.

[2] It is interesting to note that the Kuznets hypothesis also goes a long way toward explaining "global inequality"—understood as inequality not across countries, but across all individuals in the world—over the last two centuries. Due to the large cross-country differences in global inequality, patterns are driven more by mean differences in income across countries than by changes in distribution within each country. It is estimated that the world in the early 1800s was much more equal—though almost uniformly poor—until industrialization in developed countries increased global inequality. Between the early 1900s and about 1980, global inequality increased as the income of rich countries grew (even though inequality was decreasing within rich countries, global inequality rose, because even low-income families in rich countries are at the top of world income distributions). In the last few decades, global inequality has decreased again with the growth of relatively poor countries, particularly China (van Zanden et al., 2014; Bourguignon and Morrisson, 2002). Lakner and Milanovic (2013) calculated global inequality and estimated that the Gini coefficient (and inequality) fell from about 0.73 to 0.71 between 1988 and 2008.

[3] Latin America has been the notable exception in the world and has achieved reductions in inequality (Lopez-Calva and Lustig, 2010). This can only partially be explained by social policy marked by the growth of pro-poor Conditional Cash Transfers. A decline in the skilled versus unskilled wage differential has played a major role in that region.

Figure 3.1
Long-Term Inequality in Developed Countries

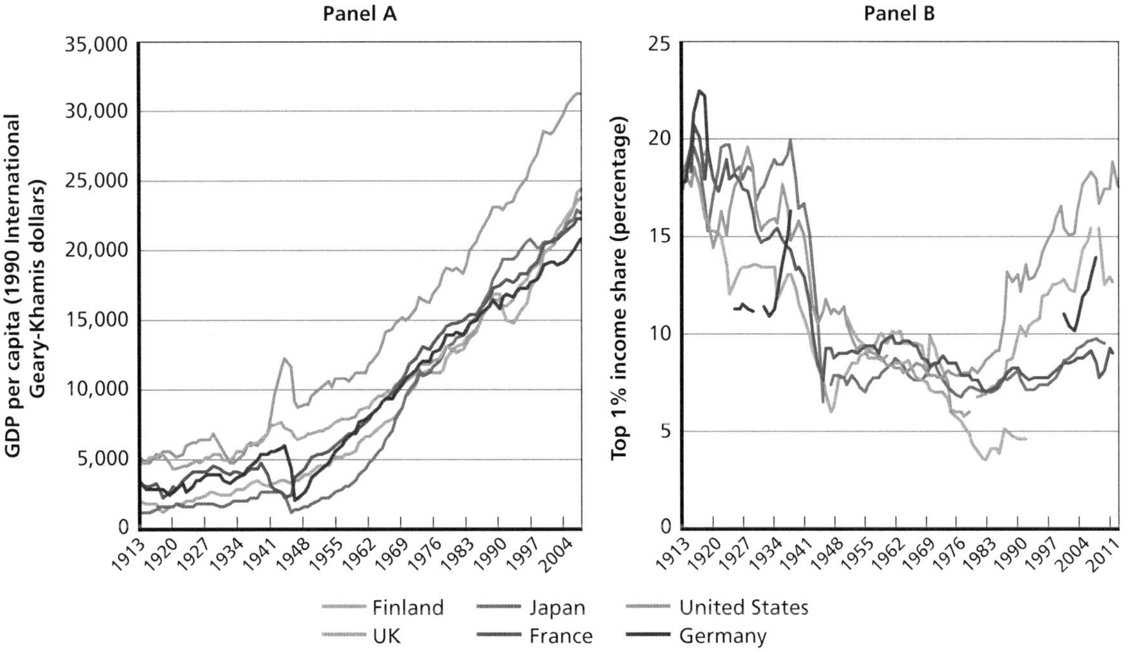

SOURCES: Panel A: The Maddison Project, 2013 version; Panel B: World Top Income Database.
RAND *RR1509-3.1*

Trends in Income Inequality Since the 1980s

Although, as discussed above, the level of inequality in the United States was stable or declining for the first few decades of the postwar period, this trend reversed at some point around 1980. This pattern is similar for income and consumption inequality at both the individual and household levels. For the United States, Cutler and Katz (1992) and Karoly (1992) show that, under a complete set of measures, inequality of labor earnings increased substantially during the 1980s, as did household income inequality. Similar patterns in income inequality hold for most countries in the developed world.

Household Income Inequality

Disposable household income inequality has increased since the mid-1970s.[4] Figure 3.2 shows that the Gini coefficient went from 0.31 in 1979 to 0.38 in 2013, according to the Luxembourg

[4] The Luxembourg Income Study bottom codes the inequality at 1 percent of mean equivalized income and top codes the median of the nonequivalized income. This creates a downward bias in the measures of inequality (tending to show as more equal than they really are). Furthermore, because top 1-percent incomes have grown faster than the rest, this coding also underestimates the rise in inequality in the last 4.5 decades. This bias is likely substantive in light of the substantial increase in the top 1-percent income share shown below: calculations from Atkinson, Piketty, and Saez (2011) show that, if the Gini coefficient for the rest of the population is 40 percent, a rise of 14 percentage points in the top share would cause a rise of 8.4 percentage points in the overall Gini. Thus, the increase shown in the series here would be more than twice as pronounced if we accounted for top 1-percent income growth.

Wealth Accumulation and Inequality

In his 2014 book, *Capital in the Twenty-First Century*, Thomas Piketty describes the historical trends of wealth concentration and shows that, following the same pattern of overall inequality, wealth concentration in developed countries has steadily increased since the later decades of the 20th century, after declining between the 1930s and 1960s. The decline in wealth concentration in the interwar periods, which was particularly marked in continental Europe, can be explained by a combination of factors, including the destruction of physical capital and public policy (such as higher tax rates). The increase in wealth concentration since the 1980s mirrors the rise of income inequality (analyzed in detail in the following section). The analysis of Saez and Zucman (2014) estimates that in 2012 the top 10 percent of households in the United States owned more than 75 percent of all household wealth. Returns on wealth or capital constitute approximately one-third of the income in the economy. This return to capital generally consists of rents, dividends, capital gains, and so on (though, in some cases, entrepreneurial income contains elements of both labor and capital income). Thus, capital income is an important source of income for wealthy households.

Given the distribution of wealth, it is unsurprising that the percentage of income derived from labor (and hence capital) varies substantially across the income distribution. In 2013, labor provided most of total market income for those on the bottom rungs of the income ladder, but it decreases at the very top: 75 percent of income for those in the top 10 percent, 55 percent for the top 1 percent, 42 percent for the top 0.1 percent, and 33 percent for the top 0.01 percent, according to the World Top Income Database (WTID), based on Internal Revenue Service data on tax filers.

Piketty (2014) argues that concentration of capital relative to overall income growth in developed countries will likely increase in the future, particularly when the economy is growing slowly. His argument is that, when the return to capital is higher than the overall rate of economic growth, capital owners will see their fortunes grow faster than the economy, which will result in further capital concentration. Whether this holds true, however, depends on several factors in addition to growth, including the effect of future technological change on the relative demand for different types of skill and capital; public policies, including tax rates; and overall growth in educational attainment.

Income Study. Income of those in the top decile went from 4.5 times the income of those in the 10th percentile in 1979 to 5.8 times in 2013.

Panel A of Figure 3.3 shows the average market income of families[5] at different percentile levels, according to the WTID. There are some relatively small fluctuations as part of business cycles, but the general trends are clear. Income of the top 5 percent of households roughly doubled, while income of the bottom 90 percent remained mostly stable during the same period.

[5] Families are defined as tax units in this data series. The tax data used are available only for "tax-filing units" (in a few cases, members of the same family or household may file separate tax returns). However, the trends observed in this series are roughly corroborated by census and survey data, as shown later.

Figure 3.2
U.S. Income Inequality Measures Since the Mid-1970s

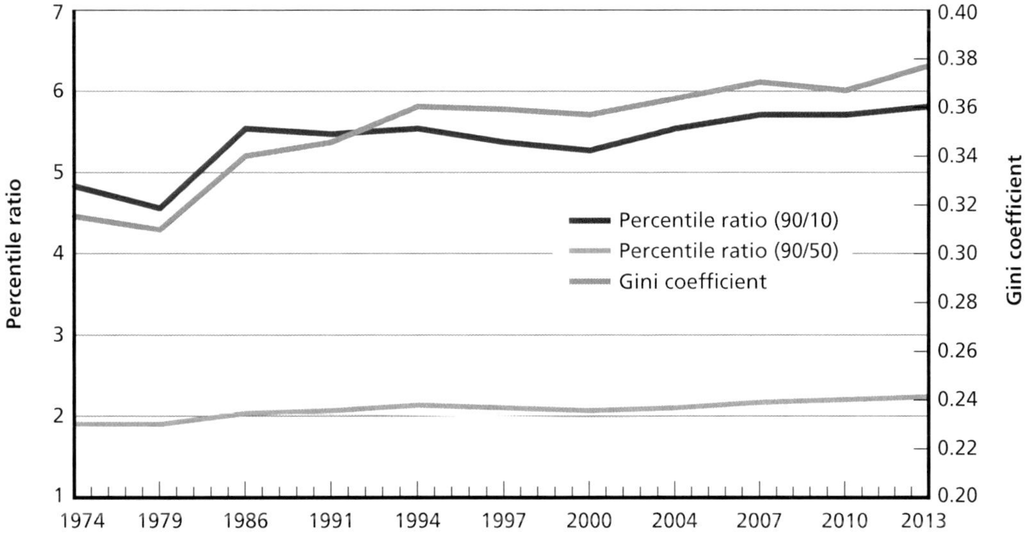

SOURCE: Luxembourg Income Study for Gini coefficient at the household level.
NOTE: The figure shows Gini coefficients (on the left axis) and income shares (on the right axis).
RAND *RR1509-3.2*

Thus, while the average income of households in the top 5 percent was approximately five times the amount of the average of households in the bottom 90 percent in 1970, it was close to 10 times in 2014. Income growth within the top 1 percent was more rapid, with incomes nearly tripling (180 percent growth) over the period. Panel B shows the growth rates of incomes within the top 1 percent. Panel B also shows market income excluding capital gains, though the pattern would be similar (though slightly steeper) if they were included.[6]

The lack of market income growth for the bottom 90 percent, as shown in Figure 3.3, does not necessarily mean that the welfare of those at the bottom has not improved; these estimates do not account for changes in household size or changes in nontaxable income (including monetary and in-kind transfers from public programs). To get a more consistent measure of income over time, the Congressional Budget Office (CBO) produces a statistical series that compares equivalized income across households of different sizes: Each household's income is divided by the square root of the number of household residents. Using this measure, growth in the bottom quintile equaled 23.2 percent instead of -2 percent.[7]

---

[6] It is customary to use the series excluding capital gains, since including them increases the year-to-year variation in income. The reason for this is that tax filers can often choose when to declare the capital gains and will likely do so when it is advantageous for tax purposes. Thus, some years tend to concentrate an artificially high proportion of reported capital gains. For long-term trends, however, this does not cause substantial differences.

[7] Another difference with the measures presented above is that the CBO's measure of before-tax income inequality includes all market income reported on tax returns, plus other sources of cash income (in addition to Census and WTID data sets, such as child support and employees' contributions to 401(k) retirement plans). It can also be argued (Deaton, 2013) that price indexes do not fully take into account technological improvements that did not exist decades ago. Thus, even in periods when income did not increase, some could argue that welfare still increased for most of the population. In addition, though income has stagnated for the bottom parts of the population, when government benefits are fully accounted for, poverty has actually fallen (see subsection "Inequality at the Bottom of the Distribution: Public Transfers

Figure 3.3
Household Market Income Growth for Top and Bottom Households
Panel A. Average Income

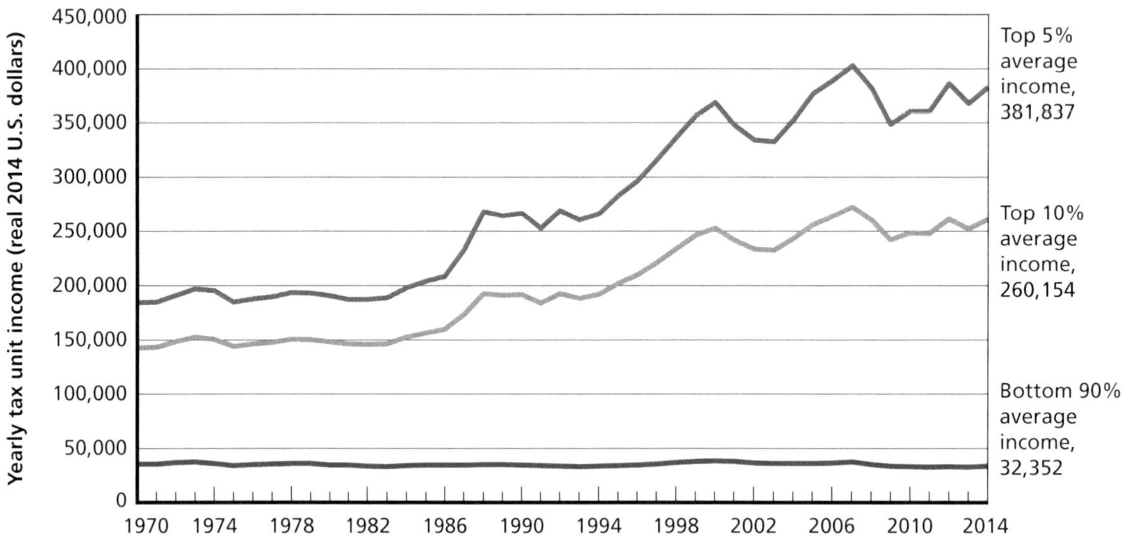

RAND *RR1509-3.3*

Panel B. Growth of Market Income Excluding Capital Gains

Income Cohort	1970s (%)	1980s (%)	1990s (%)	2000–2014 (%)	1970–2014 (%)
Top 0.01%	24.4	205.4	85.1	3.6	728.3
Top 0.1%	14.9	140.5	73.2	–0.8	374.7
Top 1%	4.6	73.9	51.2	2.2	180.8
Top 5%	3.6	40.0	38.6	3.8	108.6
Top 10%	4.1	29.4	32.1	3.3	83.9
Bottom 90%	–2.2	–0.2	10.7	–12.4	-5.3

SOURCE: World Top Income Database.
NOTE: Total income excluding capital gains.

Table 3.1 shows the 1980–2011 cumulative growth in income for the bottom quintile, according to U.S. Census data (nonequivalized) and the CBO's definition of equivalized income. After correction for household size, there has actually been some growth in market income for the bottom percentiles. However, this correction does not affect the major trend of an increase in inequality. The Gini coefficient has grown by about the same amount, irrespective of the CBO's correction.

Burkhauser, Larrimore, and Simon (2012) deconstruct the 1979–2007 differences in changes in inequality observed when using pretax, pretransfer income (the most unequal)

and Poverty"). This does not invalidate, however, the point that top family incomes have risen much more than bottom ones.

Table 3.1
Inequality and Income Growth of the Bottom 20 Percent of Households Using Alternative Income Measures

	Census (nonequivalized market income)	CBO (equivalized market income)
Cumulative growth (lowest quintile, bottom 20%) 1979–2010	–2.0%	23.2%
Gini coefficient 1979	0.404	0.48
Gini coefficient 2011	0.477	0.59
Percentage growth in Gini	18.1%	22.9%

SOURCE: U.S. Census, 2014, and CBO, 2014.

versus household-size-adjusted posttax and transfer income, using Current Population Survey data. Their findings confirm that the negative growth observed when using pretax and transfer income at the tax-filing unit level (–33 percent) disappears when looking at household-size-adjusted income and is larger when looking, in addition, at posttax and posttransfer income (+15 percent). Similarly, the close to zero growth in market income for the middle-quintile tax-filing unit (2.2 percent) becomes substantial when adjusting for household size, and even larger when looking at after-tax and posttransfer income (29.5 percent). However, this correction also applies to households in the top quintiles, so that inequality grew substantially regardless of the income series used. They estimate the Gini coefficient grew by roughly 10 percent, from 0.52 to 0.57, using the tax unit market income series, and by about 14 percent, from 0.35 to 0.40, using the after-tax and -transfer, household-size-adjusted measure. In addition, they show that if the increase in the cost of health insurance is added to household income, the growth rates of all income quintiles are larger (though again, the trend in inequality remains the same).

The rise in household income inequality has increased largely through inequality of earnings from the labor market. However, there are other factors that affect household-level inequality. An important one is the trend in female labor force participation and earnings. Karoly and Burtless (1995) show that from 1959 through the 1980s the rising percentage of working women reduced the overall Gini coefficient. However, the correlation of women's earnings with family income affected inequality differently in different decades. Up to the 1980s, the correlation was negative (meaning women who were increasingly entering the labor force tended to be in poorer families and therefore tended to reduce inequality). During the 1980s, the correlation was positive (women were entering the workforce in the upper ranks of the distribution, and thus their inclusion tended to increase inequality). Chen, Förster, and Llena-Nozal (2014) used panel data on household and individual measures of inequality from 23 Organisation for Economic Co-operation and Development (OECD) countries and showed that the most important factor driving household inequality from the mid-1980s to the mid-2000s was increasing inequality of individual male labor earnings (while the equalizing effect of women's rising employment roughly offset the contrary effect from the rising correlation in spouse earnings due to marital sorting and changes in household structure).

Inequality in Labor Market Earnings

Not surprisingly, given that labor income is the most important income component, the observed increase in inequality is largely attributable to the increase in wage inequality. In particular, it has been noted that wages (and, more generally, earnings) started diverging in the 1980s (Cutler and Katz, 1992; Karoly, 1992) and rose faster for those with higher levels of education. The growth of wage inequality was reinforced by changes in nonwage compensation, leading to a large increase in total compensation inequality (Hamermesh, 1999; Pierce, 2001).

If changes in the composition of the workforce were driving the trends in the measures of inequality, this trend would be erased by controlling for these compositional effects. However, early decomposition analyses have shown that this is not the case. For instance, Karoly (1992) showed that the increase in inequality of individual earnings in the 1980s was not driven by shifts in the sex, age, education, or industry composition of the labor force. Thus, the growth in inequality cannot be attributed to demographic or compositional shifts.

One potential caveat to the stated increase in inequality is that inequality measures that take a snapshot of only one point in time may not capture inequality of lifetime earnings. As workers become more mobile between jobs, their earnings fluctuate more from year to year, which may explain part of the increases in measured inequality. Lifetime inequality, however, is not measurable in real time, and one must wait until a worker's death to measure it. However, studies have used panel data measuring income over multiple years and extrapolated that to even longer periods. The conclusion of these studies is that income volatility cannot explain much of the change in inequality. For instance, Auten and Gee (2009) show that, though there was considerable variation within individual incomes between 1996 and 2005,[8] the degree of relative income mobility was roughly unchanged from the prior decade (1987–1996). Thus, if we could compute the Gini coefficient or some other inequality indicator for permanent income, we would find it to be lower than the one based on yearly income data; however, it does not seem that it would point to a different trend from that estimated with yearly income data. Mitchell (2014) uses a panel data set of earnings for men born between 1940 and 1974 that allows him to compare lifetime earnings (or at least up to age 40 in the youngest cohort) of college versus high school graduates. He finds that the differences in lifetime earnings among these groups are in fact *larger* than yearly differences. Thus, the yearly income inequality numbers understate cumulative inequality.

Median wages have not increased in real terms since the 1980s for full-time male employees, while wages at the bottom of the distribution have declined. Figure 3.4 shows that male median earnings have stagnated, even while mean earnings have been pulled by rising wages in the top quintiles of the distribution. Though female median earnings have increased, they have not climbed as much as mean earnings, indicating that top wages have increased more quickly.

Several factors are behind the divergence between wages in the top half of the distribution and median. A large fraction of it can be explained by increased returns to schooling, which in turn can be explained by technological changes that caused an increase in the demand for highly skilled workers (this phenomenon is referred to *skill-biased technological change* [SBTC]). Other factors have included increased international trade, which has depressed demand for workers in certain industries. In addition, wages at the bottom of the distribution were affected by institutional factors (such as the real erosion of statutory minimum wages) that also contributed to the rise of inequality. The evidence for these causes is reviewed in Appendix A.

[8] About half (56 percent relative to the total population) of taxpayers in the bottom income quintile in 1996 moved to a higher income group by 2005. The composition of the very top income groups also changed substantially over time. Less than half (39 percent or 42 percent by different measures) of those in the top 1 percent in 1996 were still in the top 1 percent in 2005.

Figure 3.4
Median and Mean Labor Market Yearly Earnings for Full-Time Employed

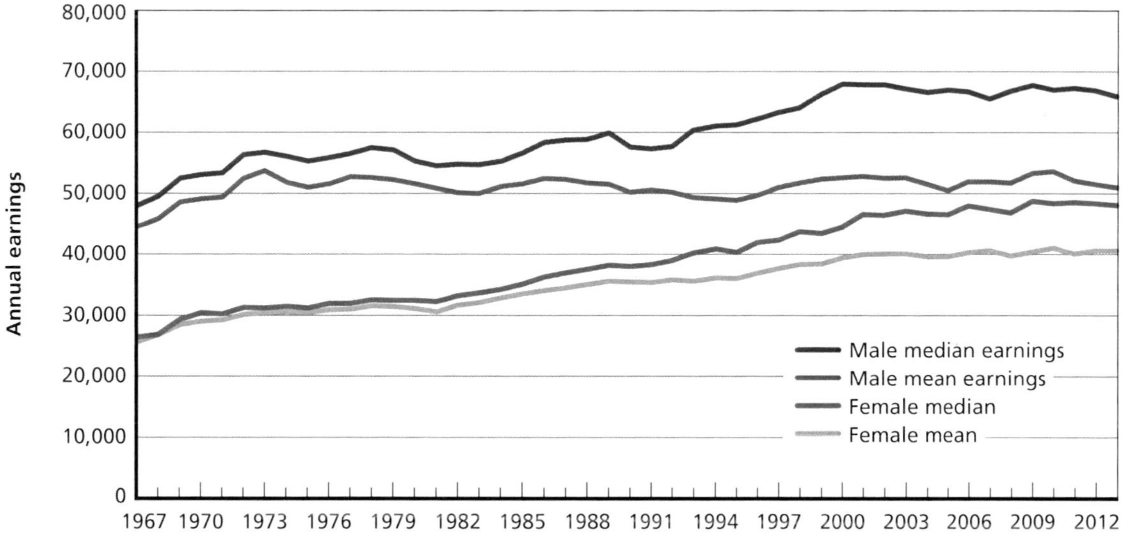

SOURCE: U.S. Census Bureau, 2014; Current Population Survey, Annual Social and Economic Supplements.
NOTE: People 15 years old and over. Earnings in 2013 dollars.
RAND *RR1509-3.4*

However, these factors cannot easily explain the fact that most of the increases of earnings have concentrated among the very top earners (within the top 1 percent), which we discuss next.

Inequality at the Top of the Distribution

Analyzing trends in the Gini coefficient, or in the average difference in earnings between highly and less educated workers, though important, fails to capture the fact that much of the increase is concentrated in a very small fraction of the population. Between 1976 and 2012, the income share of the top 0.1 percent of earners in the United States quadrupled, from 2 percent to 8 percent.[9] The increase in labor earnings among top earners has been even more rapid. Not only has the overall income share of the top 1 percent increased (Figure 3.5), but the combination of labor earnings (and entrepreneurial income) share of the income in the top 1 percent has also grown more than other sources of income (see Appendix A).

As with the general pattern of skill-biased technological change, the phenomenon of the increase in labor income among top earners occurred across developed countries. However, in this case, the magnitudes of labor income inequality growth in some countries have been much more pronounced than in others. The rise in the top 0.1 percent's income share in Britain was about as pronounced as in the United States (from just above 1 percent in the late 1970s to above 5 percent in the 2010s). In Canada and Australia, it was somewhat less pronounced (from around 2 percent and 1 percent, respectively, to above 4 percent and 3 percent); in France and Japan, it went from nearly 1.5 percent to 2.5 percent; and, in Sweden, from 1 percent to 2 percent (WTID).

Though technology and globalization may partially explain these trends, a standard model of demand and supply cannot explain the significant changes in this part of the distri-

---

[9] WTID.

Figure 3.5
Growth of Earnings at the Top of the Distribution

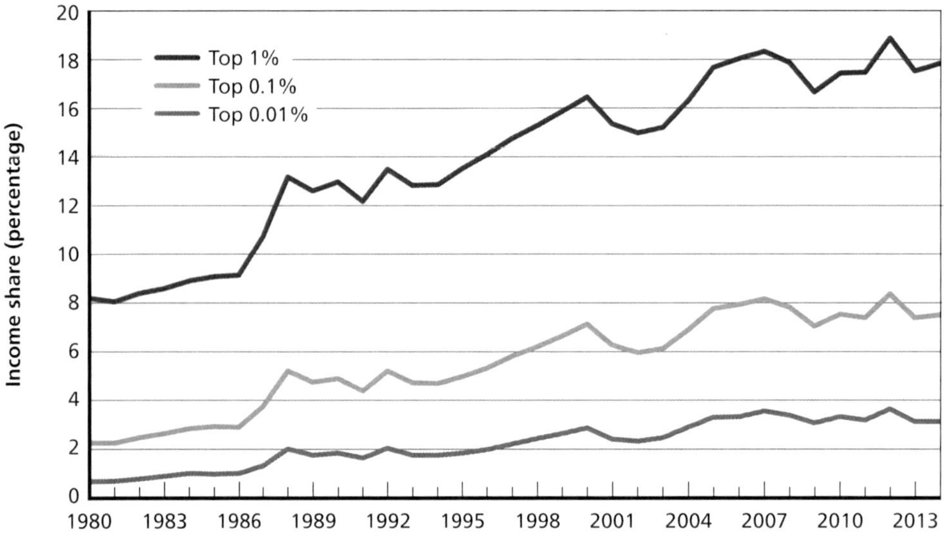

SOURCE: World Top Income Database.
NOTE: Earnings exclude capital gains.
RAND *RR1509-3.5*

bution without accounting for a particularly strong rise of demand for very special skills among a narrow segment of the population. The phenomenon—sometimes referred to as the "superstar effect," explained as small differences in talents or initial success translating into large differences in final market share for services—is aided by the rise of technology and globalization. As firms grow and internationalize, some managers supervise larger firms and can command larger compensation packages. The same phenomenon can occur within other professions. This is consistent with evidence that, in large firms, wages are higher (Oi and Idson, 1999) and wage schedules are wider (Mueller, Ouimet, and Simintzi, 2015), even after controlling for job and industry characteristics. Further discussion of the reasons behind the rapid growth of earnings at the top percentiles of the income distribution is presented in Appendix A.

Inequality at the Bottom of the Distribution: Public Transfers and Poverty

President Lyndon Johnson's declaration of an "unconditional war on poverty" in the 1960s initiated a series of cash and in-kind transfers designed to reduce absolute poverty, including the Social Security Act, Medicare and Medicaid, the Food Stamp Act, and the Child Nutrition Act, which still exist today (Bitler and Karoly, 2015). Since then, government spending on income support, subsidized or free health care and housing, early childhood education, higher education grants, loans, and job training—so-called entitlement spending—has been on the rise. Entitlement spending reached 5 percent of GDP in 1960 and 11 percent in 1976. In recent years, it peaked at 18 percent of GDP in 2010 in the aftermath of the Great Recession of 2007–2009.[10] The progressive U.S. federal income tax policies support the redistributive role of government spending: Among poor households, public transfers received exceed the amount

[10] Chantrill, undated.

of taxes paid, whereas among richer households, the opposite is true.[11] In Chapter Five, we describe the links through which these policies can affect not only income inequality but also measures of inequality of opportunity.

Though the U.S. government has pursued redistributive fiscal policies over the last four decades, these policies have not entirely offset the increase in market income inequality over the same period, as we saw in the previous section.[12] Market income inequality, measured by the before-tax and -transfer Gini coefficient from the OECD series, reached 51 percent in 2012, ten percentage points higher than in 1974. The difference in the Gini coefficient before versus after tax and transfers has remained fairly constant: between 9 and 12 percentage points. Even accounting for the government spending, posttax and posttransfer Gini still increased by 7 percentage points, from 32 percent in 1974 to 39 percent in 2012. As we will see, however, some benefits of the U.S. program are not paid directly in cash, so they are not reflected in this measure. Once we account for the benefits to those in the bottom of the distribution, poverty rates, measured after taxes and transfers, have declined (though overall inequality has still increased).

Focusing solely on the lower end of the income and consumption distribution, the redistributive effect of transfers appears to make a difference in poverty rates. Comparing official measures of poverty, which do not include taxes and transfers, with measures that account for

Figure 3.6
Official and Posttax and -Transfer Poverty Rates, and Consumption Poverty Rate

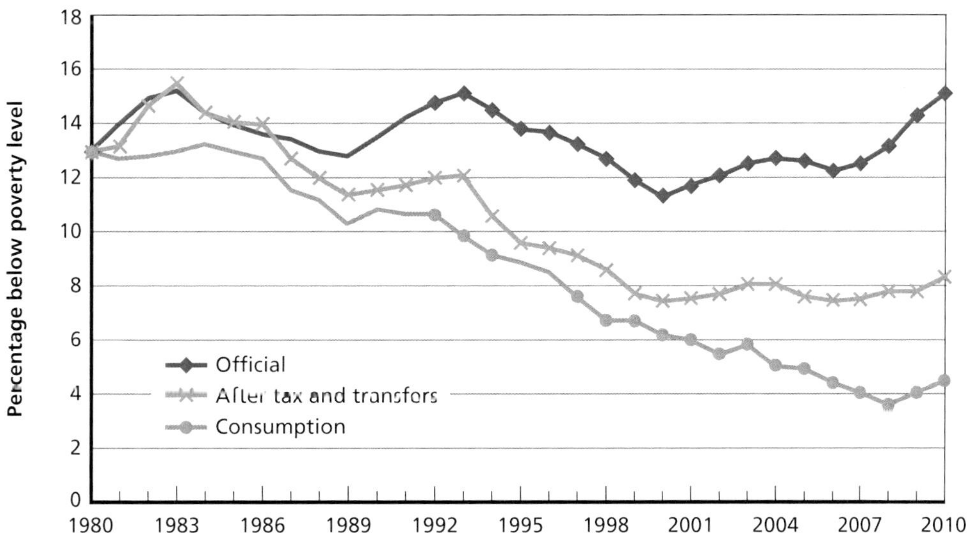

SOURCES: U.S. Census Bureau, 2014; Meyer and Sullivan, 2012.
RAND *RR1509-3.6*

---

[11] According to Tax Foundation calculations, in 2012 the typical family in the lowest 20 percent of earnings paid $6,331 in total taxes on average and received $33,402 in spending from all levels of government. Thus, the average amount of redistribution to a typical family in the bottom quintile is estimated to be $27,071. At the other end of the income scale, the top quintile paid $87,076 more in taxes per family than it received in government spending. These families paid an average of $122,217 in taxes to all levels of government and received $35,141 worth of spending in return (Prante and Hodge, 2013).

[12] This is in part due to large decreases in the top marginal tax rates over this time frame. Though redistributive policies have been implemented for the poor, the progressivity of the tax code was reduced through the reduction of top tax rates.

taxes and transfers provides an estimate of the poverty-reducing effect of fiscal policy at the federal level. Figure 3.6, based on Meyer and Sullivan (2012), shows the percentage of the U.S. population with incomes below the official poverty level, the percentage below the poverty level when taxes and transfer programs are taken into account, and the percentage of the population consuming below the poverty threshold.[13] The official poverty rate based on income has drifted between 11 percent and 15 percent since the 1980s. In contrast, when poverty measures account for federal taxes and transfer programs, poverty continued to decline until around 2000. The decline is steeper when estimates are based on consumption measures, which are more sensitive to benefits paid in-kind.

Given the lack of growth in wages at the bottom of the distribution, government programs, rather than earnings, have been responsible for much of the decline in poverty. Analysis in Meyer and Sullivan (2012) cites Social Security and tax changes, such as the Earned Income Tax Credit, for reductions in poverty during the 1990s.[14]

Summary of Income Inequality Trends and Their Implications for Welfare and Intergenerational Mobility

During the 20th century, most American families accumulated human and physical capital, which helped the economy not only grow but also grow in a way that benefited large swaths of the population. Broad capital accumulation reduces inequality and grows the economy in two ways: First, the accumulation of skill means that people at the middle and bottom of the distribution amass profitable assets and thus increase their incomes, closing the inequality gap with higher-income families that possess more of those skills. Second, the accumulation of skills reduces the return to skill (increase in supply), which helps counteract the tendency for the economy to grow due to technological change. The large reductions in inequality based on the accumulation of human capital imply an increase in opportunities for large sectors of the population.[15]

However, an acceleration of technological change and a deceleration of skill accumulation caused the returns to skill to grow since the 1980s (skill-biased technological change). In addition to SBTC, globalization resulted in an increased dispersion in returns to skill.[16] Though these effects do not directly imply reduced opportunity, increased inequality of parental income implies inequality of the capacity to invest in children's skills.

---

13 The official poverty rate compares income, including primarily earnings from employment or retirement benefits, to a specific threshold to assess the share of the population in poverty. The rate after taxes and transfers includes the net effect of federal taxes as well as federal transfer programs. Consumption measures the share of households that spend less than the poverty threshold.

14 Internal Revenue Service, 2014.

15 Though available data do not allow us to estimate intergenerational mobility with income data, a recent study (Hilger, 2015) uses parental-child correlations in years of education to estimate intergenerational mobility and finds that it was increasing for cohorts entering the labor market between 1940 and 1980.

16 Increased returns to skill, typically measured as earning differences between college graduates and the rest, raise inequality by increasing the income gap between the more and less educated. Increased dispersion in the return to skill, on the other hand, raises inequality by increasing the gap between those earning the highest and lowest amounts within the more educated group (basically, increases inequality among top earners).

Inequality at the very top has increased the most. Advantages could be transmitted for the children of this group (reduced mobility), particularly since very high incomes allow them to save and transmit the resulting wealth[17] to the following generation. Thus, we may expect less mobility into and out of the top percentiles. However, since measures of intergenerational mobility are captured throughout the whole distribution, changes in mobility for a small sector of the population may have little effect on the common proxy measures of inequality of opportunity. Moreover, the share of *labor* income within total income is increasing in the top percentile, and this effect could increase mobility; unlike capital income, there is more mobility in labor incomes.

Government programs can blunt the impact of increased income inequality on welfare and mobility at the bottom of the distribution. Despite the stagnation of salaries at the bottom, poverty has actually fallen in the last several decades, once taxes and transfers are taken into account, and income at the bottom has increased slightly.

Recent increases in inequality have been driven by changes in the returns to schooling, rather than by changes in the distribution of education, and to the extent the direct "skill-to-skill" transmission mechanism dominates intergenerational transmission, the effect of these increases on opportunity may be lower. In the next chapter, we examine the relationship between different measures of income inequality and inequality of opportunity or IGTI; though these concepts are correlated across countries, increases in income inequality are not always accompanied by increases in IGTI.

---

[17] This is what is captured in the "rentiers" prediction in Piketty (2014).

CHAPTER FOUR

The Relationship Between Income Inequality and Intergenerational Transmission of Income

A central concern is that the recent increases in inequality have translated into a society that is less mobile, with opportunities less widely shared. This concern is supported by research that shows that countries with higher income inequality have less intergenerational mobility. However, there is considerably less evidence on the trends in inequality of opportunity than on inequality of outcomes.

This chapter describes the relationship between income inequality and inequality of opportunity (the degree to which conditions at birth and childhood determine adult chances). We first analyze the cross-country and cross-time correlations between measures of income inequality and inequality of opportunity. In the second part of the chapter, we discuss the links between incomes of parents and their children that can cause a correlation between inequality in income and inequality in opportunity.

Some have argued that greater income inequality *causes* greater inequality of opportunity. For instance, OECD (2011) argues that income inequality "can stifle upward social mobility, making it harder for talented and hard-working people to get the rewards they deserve." Causality in this case is hard to establish, since both income inequality and inequality of opportunity are results of complex social and economic outcomes. A more tractable question is whether increases in inequality and inequality of opportunity are *correlated*.

Previous analyses have shown that, in cross-country comparisons, at a given point in time, income inequality is correlated with measures of IGE, the most widely used measure of IGTI. This correlation was dubbed the "Great Gatsby Curve" (GGC) by then-chairman of the Council of Economic Advisers Alan Krueger (2012). This correlation has been documented, for instance, in Corak (2013a, 2013b).

The Great Gatsby Curve

We first update the cross-country correlations reported in earlier studies and then test their robustness by using alternative measures of income inequality and IGTI. Then, we analyze the evidence for countries for which we have measures for multiple points in time. The discussion of the methodology we employed for obtaining estimates on IGTI from the literature, and making them comparable, is discussed in detail in Amaral and Perez-Arce (2015). Due to space considerations, we present here only the most important aspects, and we refer the reader to that document for further methodological details and analysis.

We conducted an extensive search of studies, of different countries, dealing with intergenerational income inequality using quantitative measures, such as the IGE, parental-child correlation, rank-rank regressions, and quintile transition matrices. We organized a database with identifying details of the report, country of study, data source, year of children's earnings, birth cohort of children, age(s) of children, outcome variable of children, type of income of children (individual or family), gender of children, calendar year of parents' earnings, birth cohort of parents, age of parents, earnings measure of parents, type of income of parents (individual or family), number of years for which parental income is measured, gender of parents for which income measures are obtained, type of intergenerational inequality measure, its value and associated standard error, confidence interval, t-test, and number of observations in the model. For the analysis, we selected all articles that followed a standard methodology to measure IGTI and provided enough information about their estimates. The studies are listed in Appendix B.

Cross-Country Correlation of Income Inequality and Intergenerational Transmission of Income

There is a clear relationship between the Gini coefficient and IGE measures in developed countries. Figure 4.1 shows a scatterplot of these measures and confirms the result shown earlier—for example, in Corak (2013b)—that countries with a higher Gini coefficient tend to have a higher IGE coefficient (indicating less intergenerational mobility).

IGE estimates, however, are subject to measurement error and potential biases in their estimation, depending on the econometric methodology employed by a given study. Figure 4.2 shows the same relationship as Figure 4.1 but uses all observations from different studies and different years (and not only one per country, as in the previous figure).

Amaral and Perez-Arce (2015) estimate GGCs with alternative measures of IGTI and find that the results are robust to the use of different proxies for IGTI. Measures different from

Figure 4.1
The Great Gatsby Curve: The Correlation Between Gini and IGE Coefficients

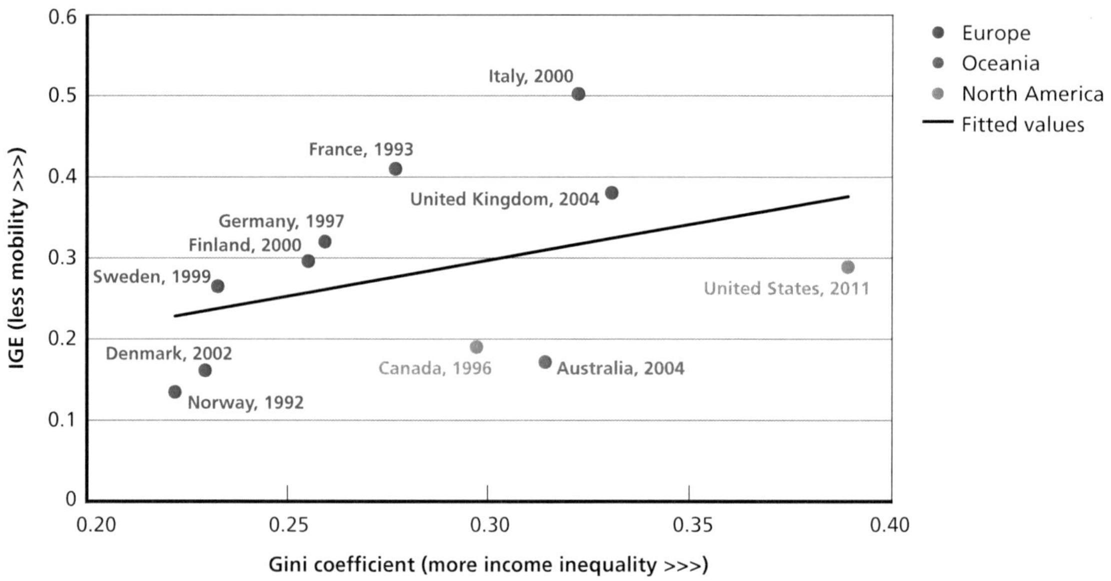

SOURCES: Gini coefficient is from OECD; IGE is from a series of studies (see reference list in Appendix B).
NOTES: Correlation of Gini and IGE measure = 0.39 (p = 0.23). The Gini coefficient used is for the year contemporaneous to the year of IGE measurement.
RAND *RR1509-4.1*

Figure 4.2
The Great Gatsby Curve with Multiple Observations per Country

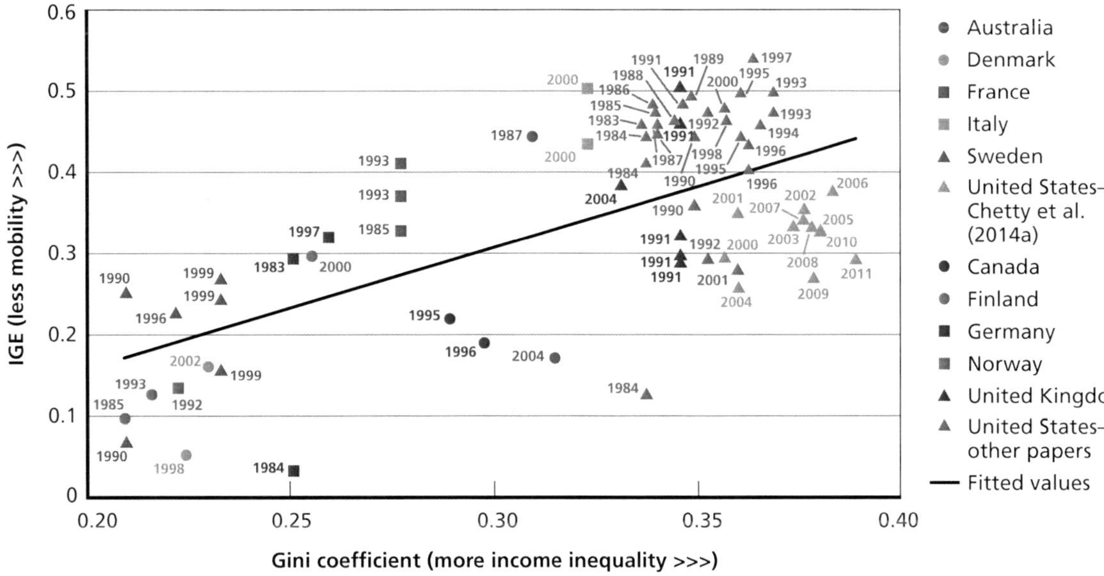

SOURCES: Gini coefficient is from OECD; IGE is from a series of studies (see reference list in Appendix B).
NOTES: Correlation = 0.64 (p = 0.000; p = 0.001 when clustering standard errors by study). The Gini coefficient used is for the year contemporaneous to the year of IGE measurement.
RAND *RR1509-4.2*

the IGE,[1] such as the parental-child income correlations or the rank-rank correlations, also show a strong correlation between income inequality and inequality of opportunity. They also show that the correlation remains, though it is significantly weaker, when using "shape measures" of income inequality (such as the share of income to the top 1 percent or top 10 percent) and when using the inequality measure corresponding to the year either in which children's earnings are reported or in which they were born. Amaral and Perez-Arce's regression analysis shows that these results are robust to including controls for methodological differences in the approach.

Within-Country Correlation of Income Inequality and Intergenerational Transmission of Income

The strong and robust cross-country correlation between income and opportunity inequalities supports the concern that the increases in income and wealth inequality experienced since the 1980s may imply that intergenerational mobility will be reduced in the United States and other developed economies.

---

[1] The IGE is directly affected by current dispersion of earnings, which can drive the relationship between inequality and inequality of opportunity in a mechanical way (Black and Devereux, 2011; see also discussion in the final section of Chapter One). If, for example, the cross-country variation in Gini coefficients were entirely driven by recent increases in the dispersion of labor earnings (*recent* meaning that they affect the cohort of children but not the parents), then inequality would be correlated with IGTI even if countries did not differ in terms of mobility. To see why this is the case, consider a society that is perfectly immobile, in the sense that the position of the children in the income distribution is exactly the same as their parents. Assuming that the dispersion of income is increasing in that society, the IGE will go up, because the same difference in the position in the distribution brings a larger difference in terms of wages.

However, it is not certain that the increases in income inequality over the last decades translate into increased inequality of opportunity. The factors behind the differences in inequality in outcomes across countries may not be the same ones that explain the changes in the United States and other developed countries in recent decades. To give an (admittedly simplistic) example, suppose that the main difference in inequality across country arises from the *distribution* of education achievement, whereas the changes across time have been driven by increases in the level and dispersion of the *returns* to education. In this example, it could be that education is more equally distributed in some countries (there are fewer dropouts, and the quality of education is more even), which results in lower inequality of both income and opportunity; but the cross-time rise of income inequality is driven by increases in the differences in wages between more and less educated while the distribution of schooling remains the same. If the distribution of education matters more for opportunity, then there could be a strong cross-country but weak cross-time relationship between the two concepts.

A few studies have estimated the IGE (and other measures of IGTI) for a single country in different points in time using the same methodology and data sources. This allows us to observe whether the cross-country correlation between income inequality and IGTI can be observed within a country over time. The trends are not as clearly downward as the trends in income inequality described in the previous chapter. For example, Lee and Solon (2009) estimate the IGE for 40-year-olds working between 1977 and 2000 and find no significant trend. Similarly, Chetty et al. (2014a) estimate the IGE coefficient for 30-year-olds since 2000 (children born between 1971 and 1986) and find that the IGE remained roughly stable over the period.

However, there are problems interpreting these results: One problem is that it is not evident which year income inequality should be measured, when the children's generation is growing up (and their human capital is being developed), or when they are working. For example, is the lack of a trend in the IGTI of 30-year olds in Chetty et al. (2014a) evidence that the rise in income inequality since 2001 did not matter for opportunity, or is it because inequality had not grown rapidly in the 1970s when the children they study were born? Inequality at both points in time may matter, which warrants a more detailed analysis. Furthermore, this may matter differently when different measures of IGTI are used. For instance, using a different data set and approach[2] than Lee and Solon (2009), Aaronson and Mazumder (2008) find a decrease in the IGE from the 1950s until 1980, followed by a steep increase afterward using the IGE coefficient—but they find a flat trend using parental-income correlations.

Amaral and Perez-Arce (2015) use meta-analysis techniques to analyze these results. Figure 4.3 shows an example of how they link measures of inequality of opportunity to measures of inequality of income. Using the data from Chetty et al. (2014a), they calculate a linear trend line from their measures of IGTI (shown in Panel A). There is a slightly positive trend in the rank-rank correlation and a slightly negative trend line for IGE, but for the most part their measures of IGTI show a stable pattern over this period. This stability contrasts with the increasing income inequality observed in this period in the United States: The orange line shows the measure of income inequality for the top 1 percent, which is increasing over the period. Chetty et al. (2014a) are surprised by these results: "The lack of a trend in intergenerational mobility contrasts with the increase in income inequality in recent decades. This

---

2 Aaronson and Mazumder (2008) aim to study a longer period, which is made difficult by the unavailability of paired parent-son data. Thus, they resort to the use of "synthetic parents" by using the Census "synthetic parents."

Figure 4.3
Trends of Inequality of Opportunity and Income Inequality by Year, United States

Panel A. Trends of Inequality of Opportunity and Income Inequality by Year, United States, Chetty et al. (2014a)

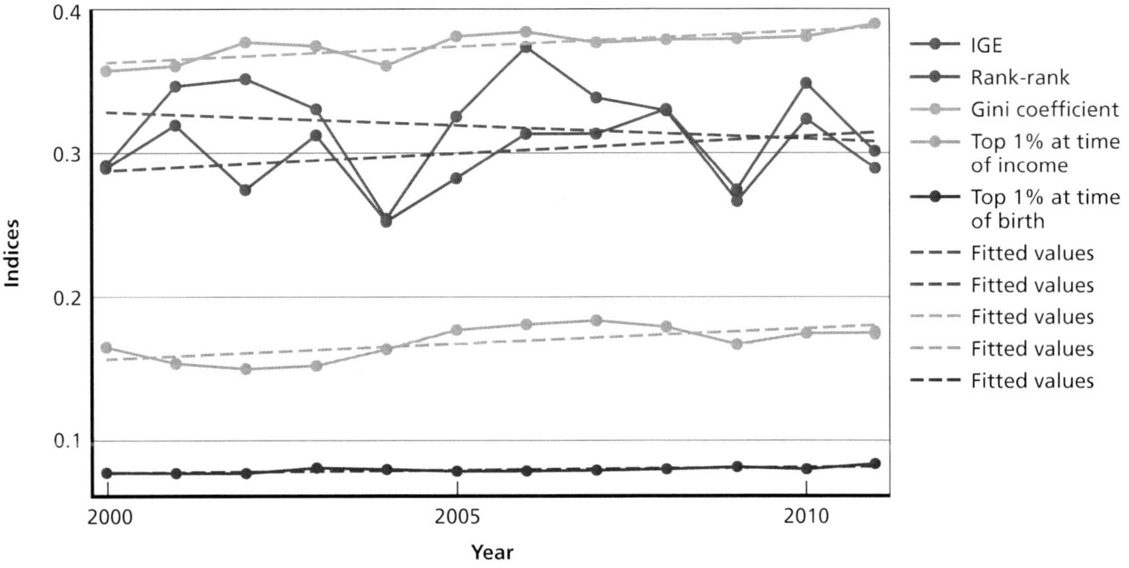

Panel B. Trends of Inequality of Opportunity and Income Inequality by Year, United States, Lee and Solon (2009)

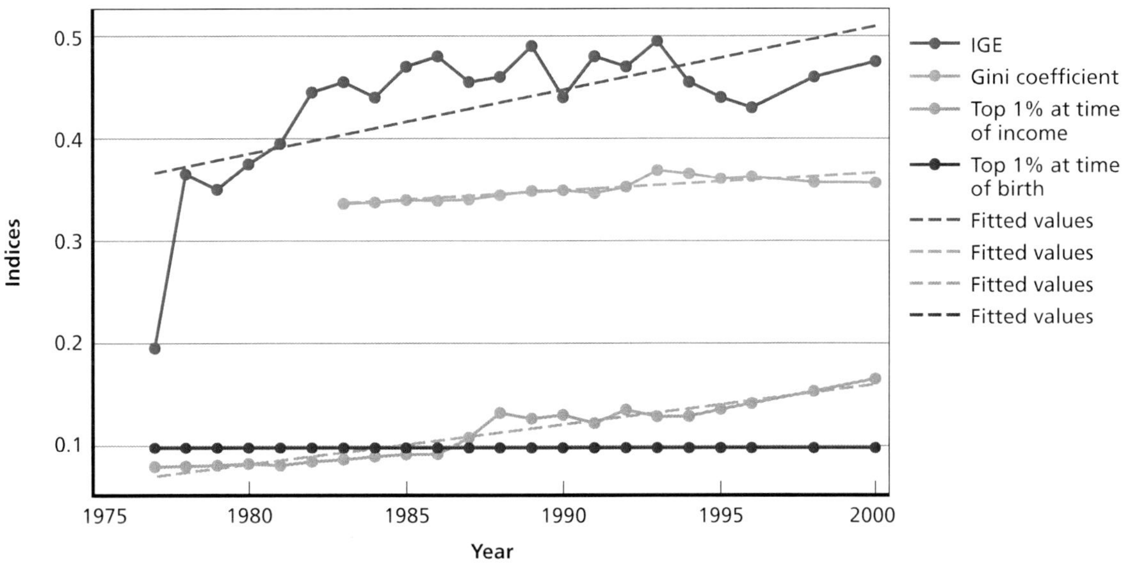

SOURCES: World Top Income Database; OECD; Lee and Solon, 2009; and Chetty et al., 2014a.
RAND *RR1509-4.3*

contrast may be surprising given the well-known negative correlation between inequality and mobility across countries." However, if what matters is contemporaneous inequality at early childhood, the results may not be that surprising, since inequality was not growing (or not as fast) in the 1970s when these cohorts were born (this is represented by the brown line in Panel A, which does not exhibit a trend).

Panel B shows a similar analysis from the results of Lee and Solon (2009). The IGE coefficients they estimate for the 1980s to early 2000s exhibit a slight upward trend. As in the case of Chetty et al. (2014a), income inequality at time of employment and at time of birth were exhibiting different trends: Inequality was increasing since the 1980s, suggesting that income inequality moves in the same direction as opportunity inequality. However, inequality was falling decades earlier, so if we use that measure, we obtain the opposite relationship. Appendix D shows a similar analysis for studies of data from Australia, France, and the United Kingdom.

Amaral and Perez-Arce (2015) make a formal analysis by conducting a meta-regression analysis that combines the individual studies of this section; they determine whether income changes have been associated with changes in IGTI overall. In their regression models, once fixed effects are included for each country (thereby eliminating cross-country variation and relying on within-country variation), the coefficient of IGTI on inequality drops in size and becomes statistically insignificant. This holds true irrespective of whether the income inequality measure corresponds to the one experienced as children or the contemporaneous one. Therefore, they conclude that changes in income inequality are not statistically significantly correlated with changes in measures of inequality of opportunity.

There is a strong cross-country relationship between income inequality and measures of intergenerational mobility. However, it is not true that in all cases changes in income inequality bring about changes in mobility. This may be a result of (1) different drivers of inequality trends having different impacts in mobility from those driving the cross-country differences, and (2) public policies reducing the impact of changes in inequality on mobility. We argued in Chapter Three that recent increases in inequality have been partly driven by changes in the return to human capital and not by increasing disparities in the accumulation of human capital. On the other hand, earlier in the 20th century, the decreasing inequality was benefited by an increased accumulation of education by large sectors of the population. These two different drivers of reduced inequality earlier on, and increased inequality recently, may have had very different impacts on mobility. In addition, public policies may have helped to reduce the impact on mobility. Antipoverty policies have helped hold back poverty in a time of increased inequality, and this may have also prevented mobility from decreasing.

In the following section, we summarize evidence regarding the importance of the different links between parental and child income generation. In Chapter Five, we present an analysis of the impacts of public policies on income and opportunity inequality.

Understanding the Relationship Between Income Inequality and Inequality of Opportunity: Evidence on Intergenerational Linkages

In the previous section, we showed that income inequality and intergenerational mobility are correlated across countries but do not necessarily move together within a country. In this section, we analyze the evidence on the mechanisms that could potentially link the intergenerational transmission of income and inequality of opportunity. In order to do this, we need to understand the links between parental and children's outcomes. The evidence reviewed in this chapter is then used to frame our assessment, in Chapter Five, of the potential impact of policies on income inequality and intergenerational mobility.

According to the framework described in Chapter Two, individuals generate income through the use of their assets—capital, skills (human capital), and social capital—in the market. They are used with a given level of intensity and obtain a return defined by the market. The following sections discuss these factors individually in an effort to understand the intergenerational linkages.

Intergenerational Transmission Framework: Human Capital

Labor is the source of about two-thirds of U.S. households' total income, and this proportion is larger for low-income households. A key driver of inequality of labor income is the disparity in compensation between highly skilled workers and their less-skilled peers, so it is important to focus on factors that explain disparities in skills, or the accumulation of human capital. Figure 2.2 showed the potential links in our framework for human capital, one being a potential direct connection between parental income and the different types of capital of their children.

We start by reviewing the intergenerational transmission framework discussed in Chapter Two, and then briefly describe a set of important facts on human capital accumulation and a simple framework to guide our analysis of the evidence on the transmission of human capital. We continue by assessing whether parental education, parental income, and location where children grow up have a causal impact on children's human capital. We then discuss physical capital and social capital transmission, the correlation of returns across generations, and links on intensity of use.

The formation of children's human capital is perhaps the most important and most studied component of income formation. A multitude of literature posits that human capital is affected by parental endowments and investments throughout childhood. The traditional models (i.e., Mincer, 1958; Becker, 1962) theorized that children have some level of ability and then benefit from investments in human capital. More-recent models (i.e., Heckman, 2007; Cunha and Heckman, 2007) distinguish between different parental investments at different stages of childhood and recognize that parental investments, genetic endowments, and environment all interact to have an impact on children's skills.

The complex nature of these relationships leads Heckman (2007) to declare: "The nature versus nurture distinction, although traditional, is obsolete. The modern literature on epigenetic expression and gene environment interactions teaches us that the sharp distinction between acquired skills and ability featured in the early human capital literature is not tenable. Additive 'nature' and 'nurture' models, although traditional and still used in many studies of heritability and family influence, mischaracterize gene-environment interactions."

There are important facts with which a theory of human capital needs to be consistent. These facts need to be used to assess the evidence on the impact of policies on human capital and their impact on intergenerational transmission of income.

1. *Health and human capital are strongly related, and health very early on is a determinant for future outcomes.* For example, Black, Devereux, and Salvanes (2007) show a strong correlation between health outcomes at birth and long-term outcomes by analyzing siblings and twins. They find that higher birth weight is associated with increases in adult height, IQ, earnings, and birth weight of the subjects' own children.

2. *Gaps in health status arise early in life and expand throughout childhood.* Case, Fertig, and Paxson (2005) show that family income gradients in child health status emerge early and widen with age. There is a strong link between poor physical health during childhood—and even in-utero—and outcomes in later adulthood (Case, Fertig, and Paxson, 2005; Case,

Lubotsky, and Paxson, 2002; and Currie and Stabile, 2003). Furthermore, Smith and Smith (2010) show that psychological problems during childhood also reduce overall educational attainment and earnings in adulthood. Currie et al. (2010) compare siblings' outcomes and find that health problems in early childhood are significant predictors of young adult outcomes.

3. *Health gaps, from early in life, are at least partially a consequence of environmental and socioeconomic conditions.* Ample evidence shows that environment, even in utero, has long-lasting impacts on health, education, and labor-market outcomes. For example, Almond (2006) finds that in-utero exposure to a 20th-century influenza pandemic had long-term impacts. Those born in areas harder hit by the pandemic grew up to earn wages between 5 percent and 9 percent lower than those in less affected areas. Almond and Currie (2011) review the growing body of evidence about environmental effects in utero and long-term outcomes.

Recent work (Hair et al., 2015) shows that children who grow up in poverty lose gray matter in certain areas of the brain; in particular, children who grew up below 1.5 times the poverty level were shown to have lower levels of gray matter in "areas of the brain associated with school readiness skills." It has also been shown that children who grow up in stressful conditions accumulate cortisol in the brain, which affects later abilities (Walker et al., 2011). Currie and Stabile (2003), for example, find that children from low-income families are more likely to experience more-frequent poor health and lower test scores. Walker et al. (2011) present a range of evidence on mechanisms through which poverty in childhood affects later health and abilities.

4. *Cognitive skill gaps across socioeconomic groups appear early on and widen throughout childhood.* There is ample evidence that ability gaps between individuals and across socioeconomic groups open up at early ages for both cognitive and noncognitive skills. For instance, Figure 4.4 shows gaps in math scores, as measured by the children of the National Survey of

Figure 4.4
Math Test Score Gaps by Family Income Quintile

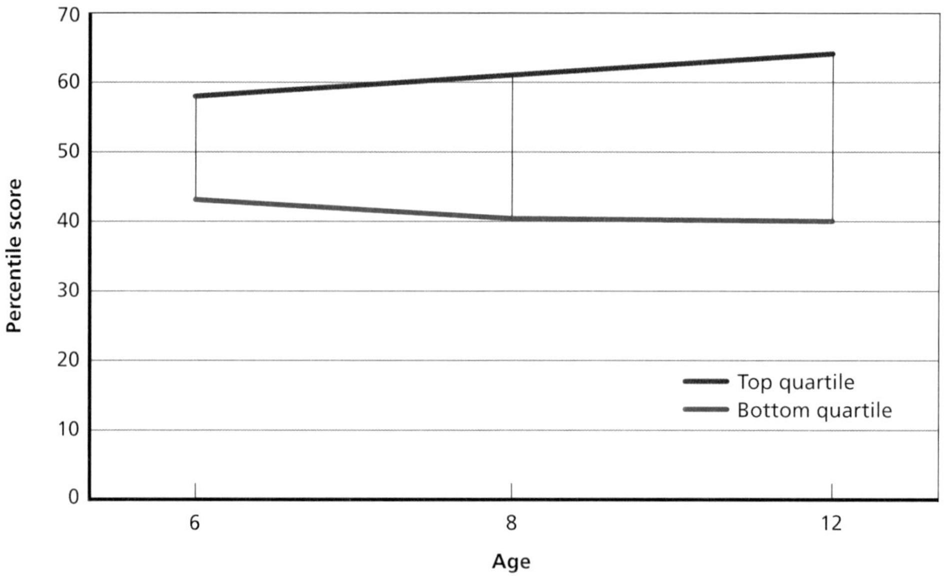

SOURCE: Cunha and Heckman (2007) (based on NLSY data), online appendix.
NOTE: Family income is calculated at ages six and ten.
RAND *RR1509-4.4*

Youth of 1979, from ages six to 12. The large gap observed at age six continues growing at least until age 12.

5. *Investments in early childhood education can influence cognitive and noncognitive skills and have impacts on future education and further human capital accumulation.* Long-term follow-ups of successful early childhood interventions have shown long-term impacts. (For instance, evaluation of the Perry Preschool and the Abecedarian preschools have shown sustained gains in noncognitive skills, educational attainment, and labor market earnings [Campbell et al., 2002; Heckman et al., 2010]. Gertler et al. [2014] find that an early childhood stimulation program of growth-stunted toddlers in Jamaica resulted in their catching up in terms of labor-market earnings and education attainment when in their twenties.)

6. *Human capital comprises more than cognitive skills, so programs that fail to permanently raise measures of hard skills, such as IQ, do not necessarily imply null impacts on human capital.* This is important, since, as we discuss in the following chapter, some evaluations of preschool programs show short-lived impacts on cognitive skills but long-term impacts on noncognitive skills and economic outcomes (for example, Heckman et al., 2010, for Perry preschool and Puma et al., 2010, for Head Start).

7. *Different skills may be more malleable at different points in time.* For instance, Cunha and Heckman (2007) argue that noncognitive skills are more malleable in adolescence, while cognitive skills are malleable only in childhood.

8. *To be consistent with the epigenetics findings, it is important to allow for the possibility of interactions between genetic endowments and environmental factors.* Models where genetic endowments and environmental factors enter only additively are not appropriate.

To guide the discussion in the following sections, we propose a very simple framework of human capital accumulation that allows consistency with the points above. In this framework, human capital has three dimensions: cognitive skills, noncognitive skills, and health. At birth, human capital is determined by a genetic endowment and by the environment in utero. We can represent genetics and the environment as "investments" while in utero and during childhood.[3]

We now turn to a discussion of evidence on the magnitude of causal effects of parents' education and income on their children's human capital.

Evidence on Links of Human Capital: The Effect of Parents' Human Capital on Children's Human Capital

Children of higher-income parents grow up to have higher levels of human capital. Correlations between years of schooling for parents and children vary across countries: Hertz et al. (2007) estimate correlations for a large number of countries and find that correlation varies,

---

3 We can represent this as follows: At any given time, human capital is a vector of cognitive skills (c_t), noncognitive skills (nc_t), and health (h_t): $HCt=\{c_t,nc_t,ht\}$. We can represent the genetic endowment by {a} and human capital at birth (t = 1) by $HC_1=f_1(a,I_0)$. At other times, t, the function is given $HC_t=\{c_t,nc_t,h_t\} = f_t(HC_{t-1},I_{t-1})$. Thus, human capital growth at any given time is affected by its development up to that stage. It is also important to note that it is not necessarily the case that investments at different times are perfect substitutes; it may be that investments at certain "critical" times cannot be compensated for or that it is "costly" to compensate for them in the sense that it may take a greater investment at a later time to compensate for investments not made earlier on. This framework allows for interpreting different sources of evidence on the links between parental income, human capital, and environment and the outcomes for children. In particular, it shows that evidence on effects on health and cognitive skills at childhood are valuable in terms of understanding human capital formation.

from relatively low numbers (0.31 in Denmark and Malaysia) to 0.54 in Italy and 0.60 in Chile; in the United States, it is around 0.46.

However, this relationship does not imply that a policy that increases the educational attainment of one generation will necessarily increase the level of the next. The correlation described above does not necessarily imply a causal effect of parental education on that of children. The correlation can have a component beyond the causal effect. For instance, genes may make both parents and children more predisposed to schooling, or they may have inherited wealth that allows them to acquire schooling.

An early series of studies aimed at decomposing this intergenerational correlation assumed that genetics and environment (*nature versus nurture*) had distinct effects on human capital and tried to quantify the contribution of each. This was usually done by analyzing samples of twins and siblings. Other studies compared human capital outcomes among adopted and biological children, assuming that adopted children enjoy the same environment but have different genes. This literature finds that both genetics and other components contribute to the correlation, though there are differences in magnitudes across studies (for a review, see Björklund and Salvanes, 2011). Again, the literature finds that the underlying assumption—that the "nature" and "nurture" components enter additively—is not valid, as we discuss in Chapter Five.

More-recent literature estimates the causal impacts of education by using "natural experiments"—events that shift the education of some in a population but not others in a way that can be considered random. The most common natural experiment involves changes in laws governing the minimum school-leaving age, which change educational attainment by forcing some children to stay in school longer. Because the laws are enacted in particular years, they affect children after a given birth date but not those born slightly earlier. In the case of the United States, since laws changed at the state level, using children from the same cohorts but from different states who were not affected by change created a further control.

Table 4.1 summarizes this literature. Black, Devereux, and Salvanes (2005) used changes in school-leaving age laws in Norway in the 1960s. They found that a one-year increase in mothers' or fathers' education increased the educational attainment of their children by about

Table 4.1
Results from Natural Experiments on the Intergenerational Transmission of Educational Attainment

Study	Method	Result
Black, Devereux, and Salvanes (2005)	Changes in compulsory school-leaving age laws in Norway in the 1960s	A one-year increase in mother's or father's education results in ~0.23 years increase in child's educational attainment
Oreopoulos, Page, and Stevens (2006)	Changes in compulsory school-leaving age laws in the United States	A one-year increase in mother's or father's education results in a reduced probability (of between 0.02 and 0.04) that the child repeats a grade
Maurin and McNally (2008)	Reductions in entry requirements to higher education programs in France after 1968 (which resulted in increased schooling)	Increased higher education attainment for parents reduced grade repetition in children by 8 percentage points
Carneiro, Meghir, and Parey (2013)	Cost of attending college (including opportunity costs as proxied by labor market condition, proximity to a four-year college, and others)	One year of mother's schooling increases her children's performance on a standardized math test by about 0.1 of a standard deviation

0.23 years; they did not find substantial differences between the effects of paternal and maternal education. This is smaller than the ~0.4 effect that is implied by the correlation, suggesting that much, but not all, of the correlation can be explained by a causal effect. Oreopoulos, Page, and Stevens (2006) exploited changes in school-leaving age laws across the United States and found that a one-year increase in a parent's education results in a 2 to 4 percentage point reduction in the probability that the child repeats a grade or falls behind in school.

Maurin and McNally (2008) used a different natural experiment: reductions in entry requirements to higher education programs in France after 1968, which resulted in increased college enrollments. They found that increased higher education attainment for parents reduced grade repetition in children by 8 percentage points. Carneiro, Meghir, and Parey (2013) used a slightly different approach and instrument for education attainment by using a set of instrumental variables that affect educational attainment costs (such as the tuition at local colleges) and opportunity costs (such as labor market conditions and proximity to a four-year institution). They studied the mother's education exclusively and found that an additional year of schooling increased her child's math score by about 10 percent of a standard deviation and reduced the incidence of behavioral problems (evidence of an impact on noncognitive skills).

Overall, this evidence suggests that parental education causally affects their children's education. The causal effect can still be decomposed into two channels. The first is income: More education increases the income of the parents, which allows better investments in children and perhaps better environments. The second is other direct effects of schooling: improved parenting skills, more ability to pass on knowledge and help with schoolwork, and more awareness of education's benefits, which makes parents more likely to push their children in school.

It is more difficult to determine the mechanisms for the relationship. However, given that schooling raises earnings, and there is a causal effect of earnings on children's education, it is safe to assume at least part of the effect occurs through the income channel. But it is likely that other mechanisms are at play as well. Hart and Risley (2003) show that children in more-educated families will have heard up to 30 million more words by age three, which facilitates learning. Carneiro, Meghir, and Parey (2013) study the mechanisms through which maternal education may affect children's test scores and find evidence that income effects, delayed childbearing, and assortative mating play a positive role, and that working mothers did not spend less time in child-rearing activities, such as reading and talking to their children.

The Effect of Parental Income on Children's Human Capital

Parental income is strongly related to children's human capital. Figure 4.5 shows the probability of going to college by percentile of parental income. While less than 20 percent of children born to the lowest centile of the income distribution will attend college, close to 90 percent of those in the top centile will do so.

The correlation could reflect a causal effect arising from parents' direct investments (e.g., paying for school supplies, higher-quality child care, college tuition) or indirect investments (e.g., moving to neighborhoods with better schools). This correlation could also be driven by a third factor. For instance, parents with certain innate abilities may profit from them in the labor market and may also pass them on to their children; those abilities may, in turn, facilitate children's higher educational attainment. The relation could also be driven by a correlation in "returns" (to use the terminology of the framework presented earlier). For example, parents and children living in high-wage areas earn higher incomes, and those areas may also have better

Figure 4.5
Education Attainment and Parental Income

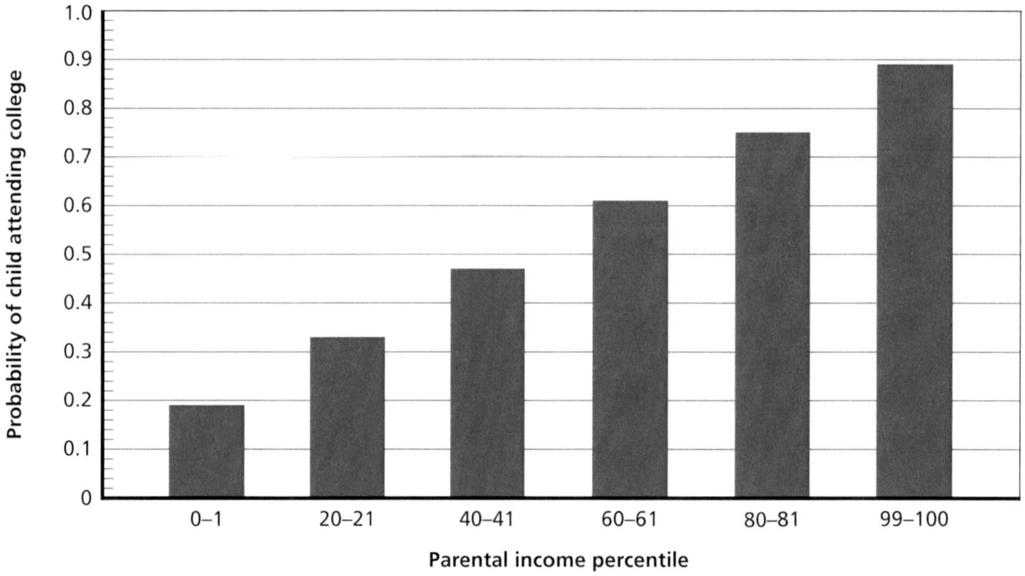

NOTE: Bars show the probability of attending college by age 19 for selected percentiles of parental income.
SOURCE: The Equality of Opportunity Project, based on Chetty et al., 2014a.
RAND *RR1509-4.5*

schools, reducing dropouts. So it does not automatically follow that an income transfer to parents will necessarily raise the achievement of the children.

To evaluate the potential impact of policies on mobility, it is necessary to assess the causal impact of income on human capital accumulation. As in the case of parental and child education correlations, two strands of the literature aim to disentangle the correlation from the causal effect. The first strand aims to disentangle genetic (nature) versus environmental (nurture) factors of income differences by studying identical versus fraternal twins or adoptive and nonadoptive children. Sacerdote (2010) summarizes this literature, which finds a role for both genetic and environmental factors. However, these studies rely on the additive functional form of the nature and nurture components. In addition, this methodology does not allow distinguishing between income and other environmental factors.

The causal effect of income has been studied through natural experiments, mostly taking advantage of policy changes that increased income for some groups of people but not their peers with similar characteristics (Table 4.2). For example, Aizer et al. (2014) estimated the impact of the "Mothers' Pension"—the first government welfare program, which ran from 1911 to 1935, for poor American families with dependent children—by comparing eligible mothers with those who were slightly better off and thus not eligible for the program. Their regression discontinuity design allowed the researchers to compare mothers who had similar characteristics but different incomes due to the program. They found that the children whose mothers benefited from the program achieved 0.4 more years of schooling.

Duncan, Morris, and Rodrigues (2011) studied a number of welfare and antipoverty experiments from the 1990s. They were able to exploit random assignment in these experiments and compare results across them. They found that a $1,000 increase in annual income

Table 4.2
Results from Natural Experiments on the Intergenerational Transmission of Educational Attainment

Study	Method	Finding
Duncan, Morris, and Rodrigues (2011)	Random assignment from a number of welfare and antipoverty experiments from the 1990s as an instrument for income	A $1,000 increase in annual income increases children's educational achievement as measured by verbal and math tests (on average, increase ~5% to 6% of a standard deviation)
Dahl and Lochner (2012)	Instruments based on policy changes in the Earned Income Tax Credit reforms of the 1990s	A $1,000 increase in income raised math and reading test scores approximately 6% of a standard deviation
Aizer et al. (2014)	Regression discontinuity for mothers eligible for Mothers' Pension in the early 20th century	Children of eligible mothers attained 0.4 more years of schooling due to program and were 50% less likely to be underweight
Hoynes, Miller, and Simon (2015)	Quasi-experimental variation from federal tax reform that resulted in changes in the Earned Income Tax Credit for single, low-education mothers	An after-tax income increase of $1,000 results in a 0.17- to 0.31-percentage-point decrease in low birth weight (2% to 3% decrease in low weight prevalence). Mechanisms for the effect included more prenatal care and less maternal smoking.

improved children's test scores by between 5 percent and 6 percent of a standard deviation in both verbal and math tests.

Dahl and Lochner (2012) and Hoynes, Miller, and Simon (2015) both used quasi-experimental variation arising from changes in the Earned Income Tax Credit since the 1990s that resulted in increased income for families of certain characteristics. Dahl and Lochner (2012) estimated an income effect on children similar in magnitude to Duncan, Morris, and Rodrigues (2011)—namely, that a $1,000 increase in income increased children's math and reading test scores by 6 percent of a standard deviation. Hoynes, Miller, and Simon (2015) focused on earlier human capital accumulation impacts of the income shock. In particular, they established that a $1,000 increase in income resulted in a 2-percent to 3-percent reduction in the prevalence of low birth weight.

For the most part, it is more difficult to establish the mechanisms through which income raised human capital. Hoynes, Miller, and Simon (2015) did study some impacts of the earned income tax credit (EITC) that could be a mechanism for increased birth weight (which itself could be a mechanism through which the test score effects are achieved). In particular, they found that the income supplement raised prenatal care and reduced smoking among mothers, though there could have been additional mechanisms at play.

The advantage of using natural experiments is that they allow causal effects to be determined. However, estimated magnitudes need to be used with care, as they are valid only for the population affected by the natural experiment. For instance, a $1,000 increase in income for poor parents may have a large impact on their children's human capital, but it may have no effect if the parents are high-income earners for whom $1,000 represents a small amount.

Given the effect of income on human capital, it should not be surprising that parental income has a causal effect on child income, as suggested by our framework. There are very few studies that can causally estimate this "reduced form" relationship, to our knowledge. The exception is Aizer et al. (2014), whose Mothers' Pension study estimates that the children of mothers who applied to the program and were accepted earned, over their adult lives, an average of 14 percent more than children of mothers who were slightly better off and not eligible for the program. The increased earnings likely came through the children's increased human capital (they had on average 0.4 more years of schooling) and better health development (they were 50 percent less likely to be underweight).

Except for this study, the evidence from more-recent natural experiments is still too fluid to provide the long-term perspective necessary to understand lasting effects on income. To the extent that we would like to use this evidence to predict the overall causal effect of parental income on children's *income*, we would need to estimate (1) the effect of parental income on children's cognitive ability and education attainment and (2) the effect of those assets on future income.

Location Effects on Children's Human Capital

The parent-child income correlation can be partly driven by characteristics of the location (state, school district, and neighborhood) where children grow up. There are two explanations:

1. Location may influence the correlation between income and the "returns" to the assets for parents. This is a major factor in global inequality, since wages are much higher in developed countries than in low-income countries. Within a country, however, individuals can move to take advantage of higher wages, so the extent to which differences in returns persist depends on people's unwillingness or inability to move.
2. Location may be a mechanism through which parents' income and human capital affect their children's human capital formation. Given the importance of school quality, child care, health care, and so on, this is potentially an important mechanism.

Better-educated parents may be more aware that where they choose to rear their children may have important consequences for the children's human capital accumulation. Higher-income parents can choose to live in better housing or better neighborhoods. Thus, location can be seen as a mechanism through which income and education causally affect children's outcomes. In particular, moving to places where schools are better is one way in which higher-income families "buy" higher-quality education, and these factors may explain a large part of intergenerational transmission of income (Restuccia and Urrutia, 2004).

There are few studies that can disentangle the effects of growing up in one particular area and confounding factors. In Canada, Oreopoulos (2003) found that, once family background characteristics were controlled for, adults who were assigned to live in low-poverty project housing did not have larger adult earnings than those who were assigned to high-poverty areas. There are few direct tests of this hypothesis in the United States. The most important comes from the Movement to Opportunity (MTO) experiment, where families living in project housing received a voucher for housing and were randomly allocated into three groups: The first group could use the voucher only in a low-poverty area; the second could use it freely; and the third group could stay only in their housing. In fact, individuals in the first treatment group moved to low-poverty areas in larger numbers than those in the second (as intended); thus, the experiment can be used to understand whether neighborhood location affects child outcomes.

Several studies use MTO outcomes to analyze the impacts of moving to a low-poverty neighborhood. Kling, Ludwig, and Katz (2005) show that moving to a low-poverty neighborhood reduces by 70 percent the probability of female youth being arrested, but not males. Kling, Liebman, and Katz (2007) studied health outcomes and show that the move eliminated the likelihood of anxiety symptoms for women and reduced the likelihood of injury for both men and women. However, the move increased the incidence of smoking among men. Sanbonmatsu et al. (2006) found that moving to low-poverty neighborhoods resulted in children attending schools with higher average test scores and a lower proportion of students eligible for a free lunch. However, they did not find an effect on educational outcomes, such as school attendance, behavior in class, and reading and math test scores. Gennetian et al. (2012) confirmed that there was little long-term impact on schooling outcomes, including for children of preschool age when they changed neighborhoods. Furthermore, Ludwig et al. (2013) found no impact on economic outcomes for youth. Recent work (Chetty, Hendren, and Katz, 2015), however, linked experiment data with tax record data and reached the opposite conclusion: Children who moved to better neighborhoods early in life attained more schooling and higher earnings in their first few years in the labor force.

Chetty et al. (2014b) showed that the parent-child income correlation varies widely across U.S. metropolitan areas. Chetty, Hendren, and Katz (2015) showed that among families who move to areas with higher mobility, those with younger children have a higher probability of their children moving up on the income ladder. This suggests that access to the better environment of certain counties, which could include better schools and peers, has an accumulative effect on children, and the longer the part of their childhood that they can spend there, the higher the effect.

Other Factors for Intergenerational Transmission of Income Inequality

Capital

We have focused on human capital formation as a mechanism for intergenerational transmission of income. Income inequality and inequality of opportunity, as proxied by intergenerational transmission of income, are also affected by capital income.

Many individuals inherit wealth or receive bequests that allow them to amass savings and earn an income from it. Using data from the Survey of Consumer Finances, Wolff and Gittleman (2014) show that, over a lifetime, about 30 percent of U.S. households have a member who receives a gift or inheritance that, on average, accounts for 40 percent of total wealth at the time of the recipient's death.

The share of income that derives from inherited wealth is a contributor to intergenerational transmission of income, since the probability of receiving a gift or bequest, and its value, is higher in higher-income families. Piketty (2004) estimates that, for France, income that results from inherited capital equals approximately 23 percent of total income in the economy (including labor income) and that this income has more than doubled since the early 20th century. This share goes almost entirely to top-income earners, because wealth ownership is more highly concentrated than income (more than 60 percent of wealth in Europe and 70 percent in the United States is owned by the top 10 percent of wealth owners[4]). Thus, income from inherited wealth is a contributor to inequality, particularly for inequality measures that capture the distance between the top earners and the rest (including shape measures such as percentage of income accruing to the top 10 percent or top 1 percent). Though there is no comparable

[4] World Top Income Database.

estimate, the contribution of income from inherited wealth is likely lower in the United States than in France because the share of capital income is lower in the United States (according to calculations in Piketty and Zucman [2015], Europe's average wealth-income[5] ratio was more than a third higher than that in the United States); nonetheless, the contribution of capital-derived income is likely substantial given the number and value of gifts received.[6]

Taxes on income and inheritance are the main policy levers that affect this source of inequality. Raising these taxes creates disincentives on savings and earnings, and policymakers face a trade-off between efficiency and equity. For people in the bottom half of the distribution, however, whether taxes on top income, wealth, and inheritance affect them depends largely on how that public income is used. In the following chapter, we discuss the known impacts of a wide range of programs that aim to raise the income of the poor and examine their likely impacts on income and opportunity inequality.

Social Capital

In addition to disparities in human capital, disparities in earnings from labor may reflect differences in social capital and connections. This has long been recognized and is one element of the intergenerational transmission mechanism (Becker and Tomes, 1979).

However, estimating how much social capital affects wages—let alone how much of the intergenerational transfer of income it accounts for—is difficult to do for two reasons. First, social capital is conceptually difficult to measure (Sobel, 2002); and second, there are no natural experiments that affect it that allow estimating its impacts. However, there are some indications that "contacts" and social capital may play an important role. First, it has long been known that the single most common method of job search, and the one more likely to result in a job offer, is through friends and relatives (Holzer, 1988; Loury, 2006). Personal contacts remain a common job search tactic despite the advent of online job search portals. Second, there is evidence in some developed countries that children are more likely to work for employers where a parent also worked. For example, Corak and Piraino (2011) show that up to 40 percent of a cohort of young Canadian men had at some time worked for an employer that had also employed their father. This explained part of the correlation between parent-child earnings, particularly at the top of the income distribution.

Parental Income and Children's Use of Assets

So far we have focused on the causes of disparities in asset accumulation (human capital, wealth capital, and social capital). However, there may be a correlation between parental income and intensity of capital use.

First, it is theoretically possible that the children of higher-income parents work more than the rest. This could be due to

1. a higher preference for work over leisure: There is some evidence that soft skills are developed up to adolescence and thus can be affected by parental investment and envi-

---

[5] This is the total amount of wealth divided by the total amount of annual income. It is a measure of how important accumulated wealth (capital) is in the economy. Since wealth is distributed less evenly than labor income, higher wealth-income ratios are associated with a higher share of total income deriving from wealth and, thus, with higher total income inequality (Piketty, 2014).

[6] For a large section of the population, the largest wealth holding is in the form of owner-occupied housing. Thus, the "income" perceived from it is not monetary but could be accounted for in the form of imputed rent.

ronment (Cunha and Heckman, 2007). Soft skills could be related to willingness to work. Though it is true that soft skills and personality traits are important predictors of labor earnings, previous analyses have found that their effects occur either exclusively through the level of education attained (Blanden, Gregg, and Macmillan, 2007) or through education and wage levels.

2. lower barriers to employment (for instance, if children of lower-income parents suffer from higher unemployment rates): However, as discussed in Chapter Three, recent increases in earning inequality have been driven strongly by changes in wage inequality, suggesting that the intensity with which labor capacity is used could explain only part of income inequality and the intergenerational transmission of income, and little of the recent trends.

Second, wealth is used differently at different levels of income. Higher levels of wealth allow for investing in riskier assets that have higher average returns, whereas lower-income families need to invest in safer, lower-paying assets. This fact contributes to total income inequality and also allows higher-income families to amass more wealth to pass on to the next generation.

Concluding Remarks

Across countries, income inequality and intergenerational mobility are correlated. An understanding of intergenerational transmission allows us to think about the policies that may alter these relationships. In the following chapter, we give an overview of such policies and the known impacts on them, focusing on policies more likely to affect the bottom of the distribution.

We have reviewed here direct evidence of the impact of income, education, and other factors of parental income generation on children's assets. These results are necessary (though not sufficient) to assess the impacts of policies on inequality and intergenerational transmission of income. In the second part of Chapter Five, we discuss how estimates of program impacts, together with parameters of the economy and the intergenerational links reviewed in this chapter, can be used in a modeling exercise to assess these impacts.

CHAPTER FIVE

Potential Impact of Policies on Inequality and Inequality of Opportunity

In this chapter, we focus on the impact of policies on income inequality and intergenerational transmission of income. A broad range of policies, including those aimed at reducing poverty, are likely to reduce income inequality and increase mobility.

As we discussed in Chapter Three, policy has a significant impact on inequality—given that measures of inequality of market income are lower after tax and transfer incomes are taken into account[1]—and may also reduce inequality of opportunity. However, these policies affect incentives and therefore behavior, and so their effect on inequality of opportunity and outcomes go beyond their direct impact.

Consider, for example, the case of cash transfers to low-income families. Though the program directly increases the income of beneficiaries, it may have a disincentive effect on employment (whose magnitude strongly depends on the design of the program) and thus on market income. As a result, increased cash transfers affect income inequality more broadly than just the differences in income inequality before and after taxes and transfers.

Review of Direct Impacts

We start by reviewing a wide (but not exhaustive) set of policies that aim to reduce poverty and inequality. The review presented here borrows heavily from Bitler and Karoly (2015), a comprehensive review of the programs that arose as part of the War on Poverty.

Policies Aimed at Reducing Inequality of Outcomes

Income-supplementation policies aim to directly reduce income inequality and poverty but also affect opportunities due to the intergenerational impact of poverty. The United States has a long history of income-supplementation policies, particularly since the War on Poverty in the mid-1960s.[2]

A direct way to combat income inequality is to provide transfers to individuals and households at the bottom of the income distribution. Public programs do this through cash transfers, in-kind transfers, and tax breaks (including negative tax rates). The direct effects on income inequality are immediate, as they increase income at the bottom of the distribution. However,

[1] However, the reduction in inequality due to fiscal policy in the United States is less than that observed in most OECD countries.

[2] For a history and a more comprehensive review of the impacts of these policies, see Bitler and Karoly (2015).

their effects could be confounded by imperfect targeting and by reducing the incentive to work, at the bottom end of the distribution.

Programs that supplement income can differ in how successful they are at reducing contemporaneous income inequality. The magnitude of their effect depends on several factors. To simplify, we group these factors into three broad categories: how targeted they are (i.e., the extent to which they reach those in the bottom of the population), how the beneficiaries respond, and how the economy changes due to the aggregate responses to the program (general equilibrium effects).

Public and academic debate on these policies has often focused on how they affect behavior,[3] which is very important, though effects on coverage and incidence and general equilibrium are important as well. Table 5.1 reviews what we know about some of these programs.

Factors that affect the impact of income-supplementation policies on **income inequality** include

1. *coverage and incidence,* or the magnitude of transfers and coverage, as well as position in the income distribution of beneficiaries: Though most of these programs target low-income families, they do not always reach the poorest families. In fact, by design, many of these programs are conditioned on working, which excludes some families at the bottom.
2. *behavior,* or the extent to which program beneficiaries react to the work disincentive effect and reduce the labor force participation of the poor: The work disincentive effect of an income transfer may depend on several factors. First, all transfer programs may reduce work due to *income effects* (there may be a negative elasticity of labor supply to income, if workers are less willing to work when they have other sources of income). Second, depending on the design of the program, there may be weak or strong *substitution effects* in labor supply, depending on the extent to which the benefits depend on program income: When benefits are conditional on income, it becomes less profitable to earn higher income when that disqualifies an individual from the benefit. Making cash transfers conditional on working may lessen the substitution effects. Third, the substitution effects may be more or less salient (due to the complexity of the programs and their multiplicity), and many beneficiaries may not be fully aware of the steps where their income is substituted due to program rules).
3. *general equilibrium effects,* or the extent to which redistribution of income may alter prices (for instance, if a reduction of supply of low-skilled labor as a result of the program results in higher wages in those occupations, or transfers increase demands for certain goods, thereby increasing prices).

Since parental income can affect children's income (as the evidence in Chapter Four of the effect of income on children's human capital suggests), these programs would be expected

[3] Bitler and Karoly (2015) summarize the debate between reports from the Council of Economic Advisers (CEA) and the House Budget Committee as follows: "The CEA (2014) assessment further emphasized the poverty-reducing effects of programs like the EITC and SNAP (Supplemental Nutrition Assistance Program, the renamed Food Stamp program), while concluding that there is little evidence that safety-net programs have unintended consequences such as substantial reductions in work effort. A contrasting view is found in the House Budget Committee's (2014) appraisal of the War on Poverty, which emphasized the existence of a multiplicity of programs that create a 'poverty trap,' leading to hundreds of billions of dollars in spending with unclear benefit given that the official poverty rate has remained little changed over five decades."

to affect inequality of opportunity. The added income could reduce inequality of opportunity by facilitating parental investments in poor children, thus reducing inequality of children's human capital and allowing poor children to move up the ladder.

The extent to which these policies affect inequality of opportunity depend on factors that could also be organized around the three categories mentioned above. The effect of the programs on opportunity also depends on coverage and incidence issues (such as how much low-income families with children are affected, how parental investment changes in response to the transfers, and how changes in investment in children's skills affect educational supply). Factors that affect the impact of income supplementation policies on **inequality of opportunity** include

1. *coverage and incidence:* the number of children reached by parental income
2. *behavior:* the amount and type of investment in children in response to a rise in income, which will strongly depend on the conditionality of the transfer and whether it is given in cash or in-kind
3. *general equilibrium effects:* price changes, as well as supply-side adjustment (for example, in preschool supply).

Table 5.1 summarizes some of the United States' main income-supplementation policies and what is known about the three broad categories of factors that would determine the policies' overall impact on inequality of income and opportunity. The table is not exhaustive in either the range of policies or the effects that could fit under the three categories reported, but it shows the extent of our knowledge of the pieces needed to understand the overall impact of the policy on income and opportunity inequality.

The table demonstrates a clear lesson: Though all programs target low-income families, some exclude important groups among the poorest in an effort to reduce the employment disincentive, which was shown to be significant, particularly in the early design of programs (such as Aid to Families with Dependent Children [AFDC]—the precursor to Temporary Assistance to Needy Families [TANF]). This highlights a trade-off for program design, between broadening the reach of benefits and reducing the work disincentive. Note that the table does not summarize general equilibrium effects, because it is usually not possible to estimate them directly.

Labor market policies, such as increasing the minimum wage, are often liked because they do not require the government to increase its revenue. However, their impact on reducing income inequality is ambiguous due to the potential unintended effect of reducing employment when set too high (counterbalancing the increased income of those who do maintain employment). Similarly, the impact on the following generation would depend on which effect predominates.

Knowing these impacts is not sufficient for understanding their overall effect on inequality of income and opportunity, because these factors interact with each other. Therefore, it is necessary to build a model that combines these impacts. In the second part of this chapter, we show a simple example of how these results can be used in a model that simulates the impacts of these policies and assesses their overall impact.

Table 5.1
Income Supplementation and Labor-Market Policies, Coverage, Incidence, and Behavior Impacts

Policy	Incidence and Impact on Income	Behavior Effects (Including Disincentive to Work)	Effect on Children's Assets
TANF (formerly AFDC)	Low-income families with dependent children	AFDC used to imply a 100% earning tax in earned income up to the benefit for nonworking women, with a high effect on reducing work. TANF added conditionalities, and labor force participation grew.	Evidence of larger raises of income and improved outcomes for children (Gennetian and Miller, 2000; Huston et al., 2003).
EITC	Low- and moderate-income workers with or without children Larger benefit for workers with dependent children	EITC acts as a wage subsidy in the phase-in. Meyer and Rosenbaum (2001) and Hotz, Mullin, and Sholz (2006) find increase in employment in low-income families due to EITC. Negative substitution and income effects reduce employment for higher-income families, particularly secondary earners (Eissa and Hoynes, 2004). Literature finds mostly no effects on marriage and fertility decisions (Dickert-Conlin and Hauser, 2002, and Ellwood, 2000).	For single, less-educated mothers, EITC leads to reduction in the incidence of low birth weight and an increase in birth weight (Hoynes, Miller, and Simon, 2015; Strully, Rehkopf, and Xuan, 2010). Improved women's health (Evans and Garthwaite, 2014).
SSI	Blind and disabled children and adults with low income and assets, and the aged Larger than TANF but lower reach of children Overall, $0.72 increase in income of beneficiaries per $1 increase in benefits (Duggan and Kearney, 2007)	100% tax on earnings but benefits only those unable to work. Bound, Burkhauser, and Nichols (2003) find the bulk of adult SSI recipients were not working three years before applying to SSI. Kubik (1999); Garrett and Glied (2000): higher SSI benefits relative to AFDC resulted in more SSI participation and less work. Savings disincentive due to asset test.	
SNAP (formerly food stamps)	Low-income households (<130% of poverty line) Up to 1 in 7 Americans receiving benefits, up to $649 monthly for a family of four	"Fly-paper" effect: each dollar of SNAP benefit leads to only slightly more spending on food than a dollar of cash (Fraker, Martini, and Ohls, 1995). Negative impact on employment and hours worked (Hoynes and Schanzenbach, 2012), roughly equivalent to effect of AFDC.	Almond, Hoynes, and Schanzenbach (2011): exposure to program in third trimester increased birth weight. Exposure to program from 0 to 5 years old reduced incidence of metabolic syndrome and increased economic self-sufficiency in adulthood.

Table 5.1—Continued

Policy	Incidence and Impact on Income	Behavior Effects (Including Disincentive to Work)	Effect on Children's Assets
Labor-market policies (including minimum wages, trade union policies, maximum compensation policies)	Increase earnings of workers close to minimum wage, but reduce employment (and earnings) for some. Some estimates can be found at Kahn (2012). Maximum top compensation policies (i.e., by limiting the maximum difference between lowest- and highest-paid employees; Atkinson, 2015).	Reduce employment levels for low skill. Reduce employment of new entrants (including youth).	Depending on predominant effect (increase earnings for some, and reduce for some others, both in the lower parts of the distribution), effect on children's investments and intergenerational transmission will vary.
Progressive taxation	Increase top income tax rates. Increase tax credits at bottom end of distribution (see EITC). Other policies could include changes in taxation of property, wealth, and gifts and inheritance.	Potential impact on investment, labor force participation, and effort. After certain levels, increased rates could reduce total tax revenues (for recent estimates, see Atkinson, 2015).	Reduce disparities in parental income.
Asset and saving supplementation	Provide universal bond; subsidize return on savings for low-income earners (Atkinson, 2015).	Disincentives for savings.	

Policies Aimed at Increasing Children's Human Capital and Opportunity

Higher Education and Training

Policies that increase education have the potential to reduce inequality among the receiving generation and have impacts on the beneficiaries' children, including

1. improved income position of those receiving financial assistance
2. increased earnings of those who achieve schooling
3. general equilibrium effect on returns to schooling.

Equality in opportunity would be enhanced in the two generations. First, support for the prospects of higher education weakens the link between those receiving support and the income of their parents. Second, the receiving generation will also have more education and income, which are in turn linked with the education and income of their children. In addition to the items above, the effects of these policies on inequality of opportunity would depend on a few parameters; the literature that estimates them was reviewed in the previous chapter:

1. causal effect of parental education on children's education
2. causal effect of education on children's income.

Table 5.2 shows the most salient results from the literature on these policies.

There is clear (and unsurprising) evidence that subsidizing higher education increases enrollment (for example, Dynarski and Scott-Clayton, 2013).[4] Taken together with the evidence in Chapter Three on the importance of skilled-labor supply and demand to determine the skill premium, this suggests that programs that subsidize higher education would have impact through two channels, assuming that the program targets people at the middle and bottom of earning capacity. First, the accumulation of skill means that people at the middle and bottom of the distribution accumulate a profitable asset and thus increase their incomes. Second, accumulation of skills reduces the return to skill (since it implies an increase in supply), which helps counteract the economy's tendency to grow due to technological change (and, since higher-income families possess more of those skills, inequality falls as a result). In the second section of this chapter, we simulate the impact of such a policy.

Policies on Children's Assets (Health, Education, and Skills)

As we discussed in Chapter Four, the divergence on human capital starts at gestational age and grows significantly in the early years of life. Thus, policies that aim to reduce such disparities

Table 5.2
Summary of Higher Education and Job Training Policies

Policies	Incidence	Behavior Outcomes	Evidence on Second Generation	General Equilibrium Effects
Financial assistance for higher education (Pell Grants, GI Bill, and others)	In FY 2013, loan funds reached $130 billion, which does not reflect cost to the federal government, which spent >$34 billion for grants and work-study, reaching over 11 million. Available not just to poorest students.	3–5 percentage-point increase in college enrollment per $1,000 spent in aid (Dynarski and Scott-Clayton, 2013).	No direct evidence (though can be simulated with the results of parental education on children's education reviewed in previous chapter).	Education providers increase tuition (Goldin and Cellini, 2014).
Training programs (Job Corps and other)	Low-income youth ages 16–24. ~50,000 youth served (cost ≈ $30,000 per year per participant).	Increases in enrollment in job training and completion rates. Job Corps' impact on earnings fades after 2 years (Schochet, Burghardt, and Glazerman, 2001). Most other training programs that have been evaluated have not proved to have economically lasting improvements on earnings and employment (Karoly, 2001), with some exceptions such as the Youth ChalleNGe program (Millenky et al., 2011).	No direct impacts. See Chapter Four on income impacts on second generation.	

[4] The fact that enrollments increase in response to lower prices does not imply that credit constraints are the main barrier for higher enrollments, but merely reflect that the financial cost of going to college is one of many factors that affect a student's decision. An important barrier to increased enrollment is lack of college readiness and inadequate skill acquisition earlier on. Studies such as Carneiro and Heckman (2002) argue that credit constraints are present in only a small proportion of families.

can have large impacts on inequality of opportunity and inequality of income once the children grow into adulthood.

It would not be feasible to review all policies that affect skill formation in childhood, as that would include all education policies, prenatal and children's health policies, and others. However, Table 5.3 summarizes aspects of early childhood policies that were started with the express objective of reducing poverty and inequality. It is important to note that, though not included here, policies aiming to improve K–12 education quality play a major role as well.

One of the main difficulties in assessing early childhood policies' impact on inequality and inequality of opportunity is observing the economic impact of early interventions over time (that is, longitudinally). With the exception of some studies (such as Heckman, 2010, and Reynolds et al., 2011), most of the evidence we have is on their impact on further education skills, but not on adult outcomes, such as employment (Table 5.4).

Table 5.3
Summary of Early Childhood Policies

Programs	Incidence	Behavior Outcome	Impacts on Children
Child nutrition programs (National School Lunch Program, free breakfast at school, etc.)		Bhattacharya, Currie, and Haider (2006) find improvement in nutrition; others find adverse effects (for summary, see Bitler and Karoly, 2015).	Frisvold (2015) finds improvements in test scores.
Special Supplemental Nutrition Program for Women, Infants and Children (WIC)	<185% of poverty line. Reduction of health care costs.		Positive impact on birth weight (Hoynes, Page, and Stevens, 2011). Increased use of medical care (Currie and Rajani, 2015, and Joyce, Racine, and Yunzal-Butler, 2008).
Subsidized child care	Parents who work, are studying, or are in training with children up to age 13. Income limits vary by state and can be up to 85% of state median income.	Aims to increase work among welfare recipients. Employment responds to child care cost, and more so for low-income families (Blau, 2003, Blau and Tekin, 2007), but no direct evidence on impact.	No evidence of positive impact on children (and some evidence of negative impacts, Herbst and Tekin, 2014), which could be associated with low-quality child care.
Head Start, Early Head Start, preschool program. Targeted and Universal Preschool programs at the state level.	Comprehensive services to prepare poor children for school. Head Start (ages 3–4), 1 million children in FY 2012 ($7.6 billion). Early Head Start: (pregnancy to age 3).	Potential crowd-out of parental investments not borne out empirically (Gelber and Isen, 2013).	Puma et al. (2010, 2012) find evidence of short-term impact on school readiness (including socioemotional readiness) that fades out by end of kindergarten. However, positive impacts for Spanish-speaking children and children with larger cognitive deficits at entry. Vogel et al. (2010) confirm fadeout of impacts, except on socioemotional success. Deming (2009) finds long-term impacts of Head Start on educational attainment, health, and other outcomes. Reduced grade repetition for New Jersey's Abott preschool programs and Oklahoma's universal program (Barnett et al., 2013, and Hill, Gormley, and Adelstein, 2012) and high school graduation and income for the Chicago Child-Parent Centers (Reynolds et al., 2011).

Table 5.4
Other Policies That Affect the Correlation of Parents' Income and Children's Human Capital

Programs	Incidence	Behavior Outcome	Impacts on Children
Medicaid	Has resulted in greater health care utilization.	Like all means-tested programs, Medicaid could have unintended consequences such as reduction of labor supply. But Strumpf (2011) found no such effect.	Currie, Decker, and Lin (2008) estimate that eligibility between ages 2 and 4 results in better self-reported health as adults; Levine and Schanzenbach (2009) find that eligibility at birth results in higher reading scores. Cohodes et al. (2014) report that Medicaid expansions led to increased secondary and postsecondary educational attainment.
Housing vouchers and Moving to Opportunity	See text.		

Toward an Analysis of the Potential of Policies to Reduce Inequality of Income and Opportunities

This section describes how parameters from the literature reviewed in this and the preceding chapter could be integrated to simulate the impact of policies on inequality of income and inequality of opportunity. We present one such simulation based on very strong simplifying assumptions, which should not be taken as definitive but more as an illustration of what is possible to do. The objective of the section is to show how the different aspects of the impacts of the policies interact, and to set the stage for developing a simulation model that can produce realistic estimates of the impacts of programs and policies on income and opportunity inequality.

We start by describing the income support policy simulation that we conducted, and then describe a set of lessons learned from that exercise.

In the previous section, we argued that income-support policies have immediate effects on measured inequality and would have effects on intergenerational transmission of income that would be observable only after many years. In this section, we discuss how a simulation model could be used to estimate the magnitude of their effects.

Estimating the effect on income inequality is relatively straightforward. Evaluating an increase in an income transfer to the poor can be done in two ways: In a naïve way, one could assume that the program increases the income only of the poor and reduces the income of the rest through increased taxes. We can simulate the existing distribution of income at a given point in time, add income to a certain group of the distribution (assuming a given target group, which we can obtain from previous literature), and reduce everybody's income by the amount of taxes needed to cover the costs of that policy. The reduction can be done, for example, by assuming that relative tax rates remain fixed.

However, this would ignore behavioral responses, which would limit the effectiveness of the policy in reducing inequality. A more complete approach would take into account the observed behavioral responses documented in in the previous section—primarily, the unintended consequence of reducing labor force participation. This could operate through both income and substitution effects. If the support is means tested, as is usually the case, then there is a disincentive to working. But even when a program's transfers are universal lump sums (which eliminates the substitution effect), there would be an "income effect" on labor supply.

The specific design of the policy and the implementation will largely affect its impacts on inequality and opportunity. We could create a thought experiment where the government provides income transfers to the bottom 20 percent of the population, but precise targeting is not realistic. For simulation purposes, we build on parameters from studies of two cash transfer programs: TANF and the EITC.

From the most recent literature, we obtain the estimates of these policies' effects on (1) labor supply, (2) targeting, and (3) children's health. Then we assume that the cost of the increase of the benefit is borne out by the rest of the income distribution in the same proportion that each centile currently contributes to taxes.

To calculate the impact on current inequality, we calculate the following for each centile of the distribution:

1. the increased income from the benefit (using literature estimates of incidence)
2. the reduced income from the reduced labor supply
3. the reduced income for paying the costs of the program
4. estimated measures of income inequality.

Furthermore, to estimate the impact of a policy on intergenerational transmission of income, we do the following:

1. Calculate the increased level of health for each child of the distribution, based on parameters from the literature
2. Calculate the added educational attainment for each percentile of the child distribution, based on parameters from the literature
3. Use parameters from the literature that connect better child health and education with later earnings to simulate the increase in earnings for children of beneficiaries
4. Estimate measures of intergenerational mobility.

The results of the simulation are presented in Appendix C. It shows how inequality is reduced immediately, though it also has a small effect on reducing intergenerational mobility that is observed decades later. Though the objective of this exercise is not to provide accurate estimates of the potential effects of the policy, the exercise did provide the following valuable lessons on how such simulations should be built upon.

First, it is necessary to create a model that captures the factors in all three categories we described earlier: incidence, behavior, and general equilibrium parameters and effects.

Second, it is necessary to choose standard measures of inequality of income and inequality of opportunity that can be used to assess impacts. It is not difficult to do so in the case of income inequality; there are standard measures that can be used. Still, it is important to make sure that the measures used are sensitive to changes in the part of the distribution that the policy is targeting (for instance, policies that redistribute income, taking evenly from all income earners to give to a few in the bottom parts of the distribution, will not show effects if the top 1-percent income share is used). We concluded that it is important to report several measures or graphic representations of the simulated changes in the income distribution so that we can understand where the changes accrue.

There are no standard measures of inequality of opportunity, but we suggest using the IGE measure because it can be used in many contexts and has an intuitive interpretation. In order to fully capture the effect of the policy, it is better to use pretax and pretransfer income for the parents in the calculation of measures, such as the IGE, but the posttax and posttransfer income measure in the child-income variable. This approach would get closer to finding the relationship between children's outcomes (given the policy) and the income of the parents absent the policy, thus reflecting the impact of the policy.

Third, policies that reduce income inequality the most are not necessarily the ones that have the larger impact on reducing inequality of opportunity. Policies that directly affect investments in children may be more effective at reducing intergenerational transmission of income, but their effect on income inequality may not be as large, particularly if the value of such investment is not accounted for in the income calculation (for instance, if a subsidy for college, an in-kind transfer, is not included as an income gain at the time of going to college, it may not have an effect on measured inequality at baseline, but it will have a significant effect on intergenerational mobility). This may also occur in the cases where the design of the policy faces a trade-off between benefiting those most in need and those who can make profitable investments.

Fourth, for many policies, the intergenerational mobility impacts are realized only decades after the policy is implemented, so it would be important to include intermediate effects. For instance, we include the simulated impact in college graduation rates for the children of the beneficiaries, but other measures, such as high school graduation rates and test scores, could be used to provide shorter-term yardsticks.

Fifth, it is important to keep in mind that simulating impacts on inequality and mobility is not equivalent to conducting cost-benefit analyses. A policy that has less impact on increasing equality of opportunity, but a higher impact on overall income, may be preferable. However, given the sustained increases in income inequality and the low levels of intergenerational mobility, assessing the likely impacts of policies on these concepts is important and should become routine among policy analysts.

CHAPTER SIX

Conclusion and Road Map for Further Work

Even though there are several ways to measure inequality, and each has its strengths and weaknesses, there is consistent evidence that income inequality has risen since the 1980s, driven by increased inequality in labor market earnings.

A large part of the increase in income inequality has been driven by increased concentrations in the top 1 percent of the income distribution. A range of expanded antipoverty programs in the United States has cushioned the impact of the increase in inequality on the poor. Parents' income affects their children's outcomes more at the bottom end of the income distribution. Antipoverty programs are perhaps an important reason the parental determination of children's income (a proxy for inequality of opportunity) has not risen as rapidly as income inequality.

Inequality of income and inequality of opportunity are correlated across countries, and this correlation could be driven by a variety of factors. In particular, greater disparities in income translate into greater disparities in families' capacity to invest in their children's human capital—in fact, there is evidence that increasing the income of the poor has a causal positive impact on human capital accumulation for their children. Thus, public policies, such as income supplementation, can break the links between inequality and inequality of opportunity.

A wide range of antipoverty policies have been implemented in the United States over the last five decades, which might have helped stave off poverty and inequality of opportunity despite the labor market trends toward greater inequality. These policies include conditional income transfers, such as TANF; the EITC and quasi-income, such as SNAP (formerly food stamps); and direct services provision, such as Head Start. A large literature documents these policies' direct impacts, both intended (i.e., increasing the income of beneficiaries and the human capital of their children) and unintended (i.e., reducing the labor supply).

Not all policies that affect inequality will have the same impact on inequality of opportunity. Some impacts may directly reduce income inequality but only indirectly benefit the next generation. Others (e.g., policies on children and education) may have a direct impact on inequality of opportunity (but their impacts on contemporaneous inequality may be small or nil). However, there are currently no direct measurements that allow us to gauge the current impact of policies on inequality of opportunity.

Given the importance of a level playing field, an assessment of policies in terms of their potential impact on equality of opportunity should be made. We propose that this be done by assessing policies' impacts on measures of intergenerational transmission of income. This is not the only way to measure equality of opportunity, and intergenerational transmission of income does not capture all aspects of equality of opportunity, but it would be one way to do so.

For this report, we conducted a reduced-form simulation to illustrate how the effect of these policies can be accounted for. Such simulations should use findings from a large literature reviewed in this report. However, the approach followed here makes too many simplifying assumptions to produce results that can guide policymaking. A comprehensive model that follows the approach outlined here but relaxes the strong assumptions would provide credible quantitative estimates of the impact of alternative policies on contemporaneous income inequality, as well as on proxy measures of inequality of opportunity and future income inequality.

APPENDIX A

Factors for the Increase in Wage Inequality

Skill-Biased Technological Change, Labor-Market Institutions, and International Trade

Since the early 1990s, labor economists have aimed to explain the increase in wage inequality (Bound and Johnson, 1992; Katz and Murphy, 1992; Murphy and Welch, 1992; Juhn, Murphy, and Pierce, 1993). These studies found the observed increases in wage inequality to be consistent with the supply-and-demand labor model for different levels of skill, with the demand for high-skilled workers (particularly college graduates) increasing. This increase is attributed to *skill-biased technological change*, with the advent and generalization of computers increasing the productivity of high-skill occupations relative to low-skill occupations. Krueger (1993) provided further evidence of this, showing that workers who used computers earned more than otherwise comparable workers.

A parallel literature investigated whether the growth in international trade (particularly with poorer countries) could be reducing the relative wage of unskilled workers in developed countries as they faced competition from developing countries with large numbers of unskilled labor and lower wages. Studies used the classic Hecksher-Olin trade model, which predicts that the price (or wages) of factors of production equalize across countries that trade with each other. These studies, however, found that trade could explain little of wage decreases (Bound and Johnson, 1992; Borjas, Freeman, and Katz, 1992; Lawrence et al., 1993; and Krugman, 2000). Lawrence et al. (1993) argue that the lack of change in the U.S. terms of trade is likely inconsistent with the hypothesis of a major effect of trade on wages. Krugman (2000) explains that the volume of trade was too small to be consistent with it playing a major role in increasing inequality. More importantly, by the early 1990s, trade with low-wage countries represented less than 10 percent of total trade. Also, counter to the trade explanation is the fact that trade with poorer countries only started to increase in the 1990s, yet a substantial deterioration of low-skill wages occurred in the 1980s (Card and DiNardo, 2002).

Though the evidence is clear that international trade was at most a modest contributor to the increases in wage inequality up to the early 1990s, it may be playing a more important role in recent increases in the wage premium. Krugman (2008) suggests that conditions may change and trade may play a more important role in the near future, and Autor, Dorn, and Hanson (2013) find that the growth in China's exports has reduced low-skilled wages and employment for low-skill workers.

Other research, however, disputes that the entire increase in inequality can be attributable to technology and shows that part of it can be explained by changes to labor-market institutions. For example, Lee (1999) showed that a reduction in the real value of the minimum wage was an important factor that increased the gap between bottom wages and the rest. DiNardo, Fortin, and Lemieux (1996) cited the demise of U.S. unions as reasons for greater inequality. They show that wages at the low end of the distribution suffered more in areas and industries where these institutions were weakened. These studies found that changes in labor-market institutions can explain part of the overall increase in wage inequality, which occurred throughout the labor market.

Overall, a consensus emerged that changing technology was driving the steep increase in labor inequality. Autor, Katz, and Kearney (2008) concluded that "models emphasizing rapid secular growth in the relative demand for skills—attributable to skill-biased technical change—and a sharp deceleration in the relative supply of college workers in the 1980s do an excellent job of capturing the evolution of the college/high-school wage premium over four decades." A more detailed examination of more-recent data, however, found some pattern that the simple model cannot explain. For instance, a deceleration in the increase of inequality would imply a deceleration in the growth of relative demand for college workers (which is puzzling given the continued expansion of computer use in those years). More importantly, some studies noted that since the 1990s there was not only a continued increase in the relative wage of skilled professionals but also a relative (to the median) increase in employment and wages of low-wage occupations. This phenomenon has been referred to as "job polarization."

Job polarization has been reconciled with a version of skill-biased technological change that argues that information technology has enhanced the productivity of abstract work that highly educated (college-level) workers usually do, to the detriment of "routine tasks" typically done by moderately educated workers in the middle of the wage distribution. On the other hand, job polarization has not affected manual nonroutine tasks, such as food preparation and similar services (Autor, Levy, and Murnane, 2003; Autor, Katz, and Kearney, 2006).

It is important to note that it is not necessarily the case that technological change will always increase wage inequality; it depends on which types of occupations it affects. As the job polarization episode highlights, moderately skilled jobs have been affected more than low-skilled jobs recently. Thus, it is not possible to predict with all certainty that technological change will continue pushing toward greater inequality, though that certainly has been the case in recent decades (and the trends may well continue).

Technology has affected inequality throughout the developed world. Inequality induced by skill-biased technological growth has occurred in Britain (Goos and Manning, 2007), and job polarization has occurred in the United Kingdom, Germany (Spitz-Oener, 2006; Dustmann, Ludsteck, and Schonberg, 2009), and across Europe (Goos, Manning, and Salomons, 2009). Several Asian countries have also seen an increase in inequality, which Kanbur, Rhee, and Zhuang (2014) have attributed, in part, to technology.

Technology-driven growth may also affect the relative demand for capital and, consequently, its return—thereby explaining part of the increase in wealth inequality and the share of income accrued by top earners.

The Economy of Superstars and Increased Dispersion in the Returns to Skills

Analyzing the increased rate of return of skill, though important, fails to highlight the fact that much of the increase is concentrated in a small fraction of the population. Between 1976 and 2012, the income share of the top 0.1 percent of earners in the United States quadrupled, from

2 percent to 8 percent.[1] The increase in labor earnings among top earners has been even more rapid. Not only has the overall income share of the top 1 percent increased, but the combination of labor earnings (and entrepreneurial income) share of the income in the top 1 percent has also grown more than other sources of income (see Figure A.1).

Like the general pattern of skill-biased technological change, the phenomenon of the rise of labor income among top earners has been shared across developed countries. However, in this case the magnitudes in some countries have been much more pronounced than in others. The rise in the top 0.1 percent income share in Britain was about as pronounced as in the United States (from just above 1 percent in the late 1970s to above 5 percent in the 2010s). In Canada and Australia, it was somewhat less pronounced (from around 2 percent and 1 percent, respectively, to above 4 percent and 3 percent); in France and Japan, it went from nearly 1.5 percent to 2.5 percent; and, in Sweden, from 1 percent to 2 percent (WTID).

Though technology and globalization may at least partly explain these trends, a standard model of demand and supply cannot explain the significant changes in this part of the distribution unless it can account for a particularly strong rise of demand for very special skills.

The phenomenon of "superstar" wages is certainly aided by the rise of technology and globalization. As firms grow and internationalize, some managers supervise larger firms and can command larger compensation packages. The same phenomenon can occur within other professions. Telecommunications means that lawyers can compete over larger markets, and the earnings of the "winners" in these larger markets rise accordingly. This is consistent with evidence that wages are higher in larger firms (Oi and Idson, 1999), and that wage schedules are wider (more inequality) and returns to skill are larger among large firms (Mueller, Ouimet, and Simintzi, 2015), even after controlling for job and industry characteristics.

Other research proposes that tax cuts have played a role. Top tax rates have been cut the past few decades in the United States and other English-speaking developed countries. The top U.S. and UK tax rates were as high as 90 percent in the 1960s but were lowered to 40 percent in the United Kingdom and even less in the United States (federal tax only). The reduction in top marginal tax rates was lower in most of continental Europe. A theory in Alvaredo

Figure A.1
The Share of Labor Income in Total Income of the Top 1 Percent

SOURCE: World Top Income Database.
NOTE: Income composition excludes capital gains.
RAND *RR1509-A.1*

---

1 World Top Income Database.

et al. (2013) and Piketty (2014) posits that this has increased the incentive for managers of large companies to seek larger compensation packages. Consistent with this hypothesis, developed countries with larger cuts in top marginal tax rates have had the largest increases in top 1-percent income shares (Alvaredo et al., 2013). In support of this theory, Piketty, Saez, and Stantcheva (2014) show that recent pay levels for chief executive officers across countries are strongly negatively correlated with cuts in top tax rates. The weakness with this explanation is that it implies that top managers were not maximizing compensation when it was taxed more heavily (which they explain as a result of facing trade-off compensation for other goals, such as enterprise growth).

Another alternative explanation is that social norms have changed. Given the difficulty of measuring the marginal productivity of top managers, the governance situation in large companies results in chief executive officers having enough bargaining power to negotiate their compensation, and thus seize part of their firms' profit. In standard job search theory, jobs materialize when an employer opens up a vacancy, which is costly to maintain unfilled, and at the same time job seekers engage in costly job searches. As a result, potential job matches create a positive surplus, and the worker and employer bargain over how to divide the surplus. Since there is no way to accurately measure the productivity, or the value, of CEOs' work, social norms play a role in determining their compensation. Alvaredo et al. (2013) theorize that social norms have become more lax in terms of acceptable levels of compensation. This change in norms could be the product of the same trends that were driving a reduction in top tax rates. The weakness of this hypothesis, however, is that it does not explain why these norms would have changed.

Other industry-specific factors may have affected the growth of top wages. For instance, Philippon and Reshef (2012) argue that financial deregulation may have affected the growth of top wages in the financial sector (which holds a significant fraction of top incomes). The study finds a strong correlation between financial deregulation and the skill intensity and complexity of jobs in finance, which could explain the rise in premium in that sector.

APPENDIX B

Reference Sources for the Great Gatsby Curves

Atkinson, A. B., "On Intergenerational Income Mobility in Britain," *Journal of Post Keynesian Economics*, Vol. 3, No. 2, 1981, pp. 194–218.

Atkinson, A. B., and S. Morelli, "Chartbook of Economic Inequality," Society for the Study of Economic Inequality (ECINEQ) Working Paper Series, ECINEQ WP 2014-324, 2014, pp. 1–65.

Atkinson, A. B., T. Piketty, and E. Saez, "Top Incomes in the Long Run of History," *Journal of Economic Literature*, Vol. 49, No. 1, 2011, pp. 3–71.

Aydemir, A., W.-H. Chen, and M. Corak, "Intergenerational Education Mobility Among the Children of Canadian Immigrants," *Canadian Public Policy—Analyse de politiques 34 (supplement/numéro spécial)*, 2013, pp. S107–S122.

Becker, G., and N. Tomes, "Human Capital and the Rise and Fall of Families," *Journal of Labor Economics*, Vol. 4, 1986, pp. S1–S39.

Behrman, J., and P. Taubman, "Intergenerational Earnings Mobility in the United States: Some Estimates and a Test of Becker's Intergenerational Endowments Model," *Review of Economics and Statistics*, Vol. 67, 1985, pp. 144–151.

Björklund, A., and L. Chadwick, "Intergenerational Income Mobility in Permanent and Separated Families," *Economics Letters*, Vol. 80, No. 2, 2003, pp. 239–246.

Björklund, A., and M. Jantti, "Intergenerational Income Mobility in Sweden Compared to the United States," *American Economic Review*, Vol. 87, No. 5, 1997, pp. 1009–1018.

Black, S. E., and P. J. Devereux, "Recent Developments in Intergenerational Mobility, *Handbook of Labor Economics*, O. Ashenfelter and D. Card, eds., Amsterdam: Elsevier, 2011, pp. 1487–1541.

Blanden, B., and S. Machin, "Up and Down the Generational Income Ladder in Britain: Past Changes and Future Prospects," *National Institute Economic Review*, Vol. 205, 2008, pp. 101–116.

Blau, P. M., and O. D. Duncan, *The American Occupational Structure*, New York: John Wiley and Sons, 1967.

Boserup, S. H., W. Kopczuk, and C. T. Kreiner, "Born with a Silver Spoon: Danish Evidence on Intergenerational Wealth Formation from Cradle to Adulthood," D.o.E. Working Paper, University of Copenhagen, 2015.

Breen, R., "Educational Expansion and Social Mobility in the 20th Century," *Social Forces*, Vol. 89, No. 2, 2010, pp. 365–388.

Brunori, P., F. H. G. Ferreira, and V. Peragine, "Inequality of Opportunity, Income Inequality and Economic Mobility: Some International Comparisons," Policy Research Working Paper, The World Bank, 2013.

Chetty, R., N. Hendren, P. Kline, and E. Saez, "Where Is the Land of Opportunity? The Geography of Intergenerational Mobility in the United States," *Quarterly Journal of Economics*, Vol. 129, No. 4, 2014, pp. 1553–1623.

Chetty, R., N. Hendren, P. Kline, E. Saez, and N. Turner, "Is the United States Still a Land of Opportunity? Recent Trends in Intergenerational Mobility," NBER Working Paper Series 19844, 2014.

Corak, M., "Do Poor Children Become Poor Adults? Lessons from a Cross Country Comparison of Generational Earnings Mobility," IZA Discussion Paper Series 1993, 2006.

———, "Income Inequality, Equality of Opportunity, and Intergenerational Mobility," *Journal of Economic Perspectives*, Vol. 27, No. 3, 2013, pp. 79–102.

Corak, M., and A. Heisz, "The Intergenerational Earnings and Income Mobility of Canadian Men: Evidence from Longitudinal Income Tax Data," *Journal of Human Resources*, Vol. 34, No. 3, 1999, pp. 504–533.

Corak, M., M. J. Lindquist, and B. Mazumder, "A Comparison of Upward and Downward Intergenerational Mobility in Canada, Sweden and the United States," *Labour Economics*, Vol. 30, 2014, pp. 185–200.

Couch, K. A., and T. A. Dunn, "Intergenerational Correlations in Labor Market Status: A Comparison of the United States and Germany," *Journal of Human Resources*, Vol. 32, No. 1, 1997, pp. 210–232.

Dearden, L., S. Machin, and H. Reed, "Intergenerational Mobility in Britain," *Economic Journal*, Vol. 107, No. 440, 1997, pp. 47–66.

Dunn, C. E., "The Intergenerational Transmission of Lifetime Earnings: Evidence from Brazil," *B. E. Journal of Economic Analysis and Policy*, Vol. 7, No. 2, 2007, Article 2.

Eriksson, K., and B. Simpson, "What Do Americans Know About Inequality? It Depends on How You Ask Them," *Judgment and Decision Making*, Vol. 7, No. 6, 2012, pp. 741–745.

Eriksson, K., and B. Simpson, "The Available Evidence Suggests the Percent Measure Should Not Be Used to Study Inequality: Reply to Norton and Ariely," *Judgment and Decision Making*, Vol. 8, No. 3, 2013, pp. 395–396.

Gustafsson, B., The Degree and Pattern of Income Immobility in Sweden," *Review of Income and Wealth*, Vol. 40, No. 1, 1994, pp. 67–86.

Han, C., J. G. Janmaat, B. Hoskins, and A. Green, "Perceptions of Inequalities: Implications for Social Cohesion," Centre for Learning and Life Chances in Knowledge Economies and Societies Research Paper 35, 2012.

Hauser, R. M., "Intergenerational Economic Mobility in the United States: Measures, Differentials and Trends," Center for Demography and Ecology Working Paper, University of Wisconsin-Madison, 2010.

Hirvonen, L. H., "Intergenerational Earnings Mobility Among Daughters and Sons: Evidence from Sweden and a Comparison with the United States," *American Journal of Economics and Sociology*, Vol. 67, No. 5, 2008, pp. 777–826.

Hout, M., and T. A. DiPrete, "What Have We Learned: RC28's Contribution to Knowledge About Social Stratification," *Research in Social Stratification and Mobility*, Vol. 24, 2006, pp. 1–20.

Hussain, M. A., M. D. Munk, and J. Bonke, "How Sensitive is Intergenerational Earnings Mobility to Different Measures?" Danish National Centre for Social Research, Working Paper 7, 2008.

Jäntti, M., B. Bratsberg, K. Roed, O. Raaum, R. Naylor, E. Österbacka, A. Björklund, and T. Eriksson, "American Exceptionalism in a New Light: A Comparison of Intergenerational Earnings Mobility in the Nordic Countries, the United Kingdom, and the United States," IZA Discussion Paper Series 1938, 2006.

Keller, T., M. Medgyesi, and I. G. Tóth, "Analysing the Link Between Measured and Perceived Income Inequality in European Countries" European Commission, Directorate-General Employment, Social Affairs and Equal Opportunities, Unit E1—Social and Demographic Analysis, Research Note 8, 2010.

Krueger, A. B., *The Rise and Consequences of Inequality in the United States*, C.o.E. Advisers, 2012.

Lee, C. I., and G. Solon, "Trends in Intergenerational Income Mobility," *Review of Economics and Statistics*, Vol. 91, No. 4, 2009, pp. 766–772.

Lefranc, A., and A. Trannoy, "Intergenerational Earnings Mobility in France: Is France More Mobile than the US?" *Annales d'Économie et de Statistique*, Vol. 78, 2005, pp. 57–77.

Leigh, A., "Intergenerational Mobility in Australia," *B.E. Journal of Economic Analysis and Policy*, Vol. 7, No. 2, 2007, Article 6.

Mare, R. D., and V. Maralani, "The Intergenerational Effects of Changes in Women's Educational Attainments," *American Sociological Review*, Vol. 71, 2006, pp. 542–564.

Mazumder, B., "Fortunate Sons: New Estimates of Intergenerational Mobility in the United States Using Social Security Earnings Data," *Review of Economics and Statistics*, Vol. 87, No. 2, 2005, pp. 235–255.

Mocetti, S., "Intergenerational Earnings Mobility in Italy," *B. E. Journal of Economic Analysis and Policy*, Vol. 7, No. 2, 2007, Article 5.

Nicoletti, E., and J. F. Ermisch, "Intergenerational Earnings Mobility: Changes Across Cohorts in Britain," *B. E. Journal of Economic Analysis and Policy*, Vol. 7, No. 2, 2007, Article 9.

Niehues, J., "Subjective Perceptions of Inequality and Redistributive Preferences: An International Comparison," C.I.f.E.R. (IW), 2014.

Norton, M. I., and D. Ariely, "Building a Better America—One Wealth Quintile at a Time," *Perspectives on Psychological Science*, Vol. 6, No. 1, 2011, pp. 9–12.

———, "Americans' Desire for Less Wealth Inequality Does Not Depend on How You Ask Them," *Judgment and Decision Making*, Vol. 8, No. 3, 2013, pp. 393–394.

Osterbacka, E., "Family Background and Economic Status in Finland," *Scandinavian Journal of Economics*, Vol. 103, No. 3, 2001, pp. 467–484.

Osterberg, T., "Intergenerational Income Mobility in Sweden: What Do Tax-Data Show?" *Review of Income and Wealth*, Vol. 46, No. 4, 2000, pp. 421–436.

Pekkarinen, T., R. Uusitalo, and S. Kerr, "School Tracking and Intergenerational Income Mobility: Evidence from the Finnish Comprehensive School Reform," *Journal of Public Economics*, Vol. 93, 2009, pp. 965–973.

Pew, C. T., and F. Russell Sage, *Economic Mobility in the United States*, Pew Charitable Trusts and Russell Sage Foundation, 2015.

Piraino, P., "Comparable Estimates of Intergenerational Income Mobility in Italy," *B. E. Journal of Economic Analysis and Policy*, Vol. 7, No. 2, 2007, Article 1.

Sewell, W. H., A. O. Haller, and A. Portes, "The Educational and Early Occupational Attainment Process," *American Sociological Review*, Vol. 34, No. 1, 1969, pp. 82–92.

Sewell, W. H., and R. M. Hauser, *Education, Occupation, and Earnings: Achievement in the Early Career*, New York: Academic Press, 1975.

Solon, G., "Intergenerational Income Mobility in the United States," *American Economic Review*, Vol. 82 No. 3, 1992, pp. 393–408.

Solon, G., ed., "Intergenerational Mobility in the Labor Market," *Handbook of Labor Economics*, Amsterdam: North Holland, 1999.

Torche, F., "Analyses of Intergenerational Mobility: An Interdisciplinary Review," *Annals of American Academy of Political and Social Science*, Vol. 657, 2015, pp. 37–62.

Turcotte, M., "Intergenerational Education Mobility: University Completion in Relation to Parents' Education Level," *Statistics Canada Catalogue, Canadian Social Trends*, 2011, pp. 37–43.

Vogel, T., "Reassessing Intergenerational Mobility in Germany and the United States: The Impact of Differences in Lifecycle Earnings Patterns," SFB Discussion Paper, Humboldt University, Berlin, 2008.

Zimmerman, D. J., "Regression Toward Mediocrity in Economic Stature," *American Economic Review*, Vol. 82, No. 3, 1992, pp. 409–429.

APPENDIX C

Results of Income Support Simulation

We have constructed a simple model to explore the mobility implications of reducing inequality through redistribution. Specifically, we look at the changes in IGE and at college attendance based on changes in parental income. IGE can be thought of as the share of the gap in earnings between two people that can be attributed to the difference in the earnings of their parents. We do not assume a specific mechanism of redistribution, though we do assume that the redistribution is done through the labor market (one such mechanism could be through the Earned Income Tax Credit program) and that the program is completely paid for through reduced earnings around the threshold. We do not include any incentive or disincentive effects at either the top or bottom of the income distribution.

We used the distribution of taxable income, excluding capital gains, for working-age people (those between 25 and 54) based on data from the Current Population Survey (Center for Economic and Policy Research, undated) and the World Top Income Database (Piketty and Saez, 2006). We tested the 20th, 25th, and 30th percentiles of income as the threshold incomes where people below that income are recipients of transfers, and people above that income provide funds for transfer through taxes. The redistribution function is a weighted average of the current income distribution and the threshold distribution, where the weight functions as the level of redistribution.

Using the IGE for the United States, we estimated the impact that redistribution would have on the next generation's earnings (Corak, 2013b). Figure C.1 is a comparison of the expected income based on parental income for different levels of redistribution. Because roughly 12 percent of working-age tax units have no taxable income, a threshold income for redistribution of 20 percent affects only a small share of families, and the increase in childhood income is relatively small. Higher income thresholds for redistribution lead to a larger effect.

Table C.1 has estimates of the reduction of income at the top of the income distribution, the modified Gini coefficient, and the increase in college attendance for different levels of redistribution. The increase in college attendance is based on work that found that college attendance was linear across percentiles of parental income (Chetty, Hendren, and Katz, 2015). While our model's cash transfer does not change a family's income percentile, the transfer does move the postredistribution income to a level that would correspond to a different percentile in the original distribution. That is to say that the recipient of the redistribution is counted as earning the same as someone in a higher-percentile group who did not receive the redistribution (e.g., for some level of redistribution, someone at the 10th percentile, after the redistribution, would take home as much as someone at the 12th percentile, who did not receive the redistribution). Likewise, people who earned too much to qualify for the redistribution have lower postredistribution incomes than their preredistribution levels.

Figure C.1
Estimated Impact of Redistribution on Next Generation's Earnings

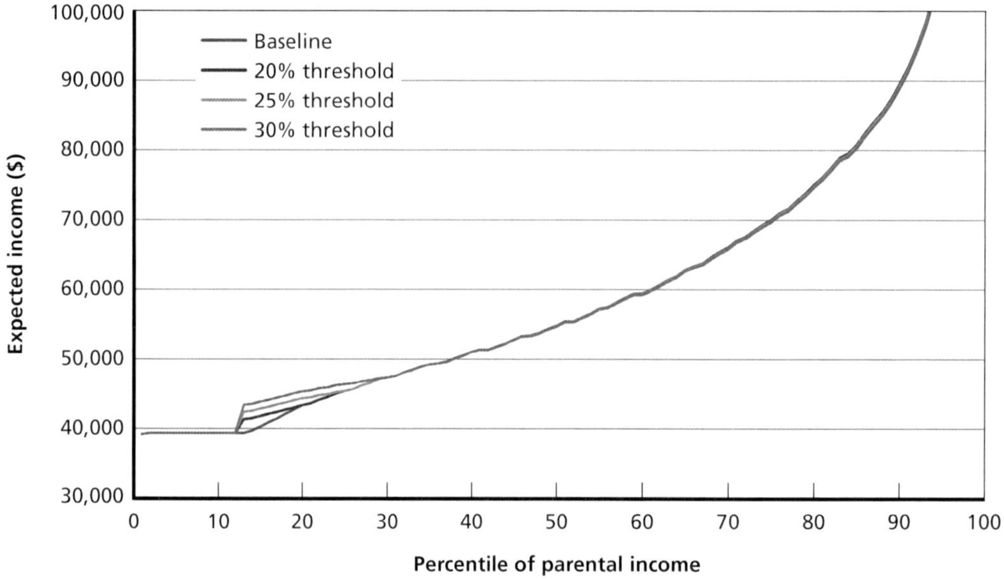

SOURCE: Authors' calculations.
RAND *RR1509-C.1*

The reduction in income at the top required to make a substantial increase in the level of income at the bottom is relatively small because of the high concentration of income at the top. The Gini coefficient is only slightly smaller with this type of redistribution; this high concentration of income at the top persists even with the type of redistribution we tested. This also means that the change in the IGE declines only a small amount. Alternatively, because the absolute income gains at the bottom of the income distribution are high, the college attendance rate can increase by a few percentage points for higher levels of market redistribution for people at the bottom of the distribution and result in a net increase in national college attendance. Thus, estimates of the impact of economic mobility from redistribution will vary by both the level of redistribution and the specific measure of mobility used.

Table C.1
Estimated Impact of Redistribution on Inequality and College Attendance

	Income Increase at the Bottom (%)	Income Reduction at the Top (%)	Reduction in Gini Coefficient (%)	Reduction in IGE (%)	Increase in Net College Attendance (%)
Baseline	0.00	0.00	0.00	0.00	0.00
20% threshold	54.96	–0.36	–0.73	–0.34	0.05
25% threshold	45.45	–0.87	–1.64	–0.82	0.22
30% threshold	43.58	–1.68	–2.95	–1.55	0.52

SOURCE: Authors' calculations.

Within-Country Changes in Inequality of Income and Opportunity: Analysis for Additional Countries

Figure D.1 shows the same relationship for selected studies of other countries. Panel A shows the analysis for Australia based on Leigh (2007), Panel B for France based on Lefranc and Trannoy (2005), and Panel C for the United Kingdom based on Blanden and Machin (2008). Overall, from the graphical analysis, there does not seem to be a consistent relationship within a country between changes in IGTI and income inequality. The importance of inequality at time of birth, compared with inequality at time of income, in predicting IGTI is part of a complex discussion. For the Australian case, IGTI seems to follow the decreasing trend of income inequality at time of birth. In the study about France, IGTI increased over time, while inequality at time of birth decreased over time, and inequality at time of income was stable. In the case of the United Kingdom, while some IGTI measures increased over time (IGE and rank-rank), inequality at time of birth slightly decreased, and inequality at time of income slightly increased.

These results emphasize the need to conduct a meta-regression analysis about the association of IGTI measures and income inequality measures (at time of birth and at time of income). The aim is to better understand these correlations in a multivariate approach. A set of independent variables can be included in the analysis about trends of IGTI measures, such as (1) Gini coefficient, (2) top 1 percent income share, (3) top 10 percent income share, (4) country indicators, (5) gender of children, (6) gender of parents, (7) number of years for which parents' earnings are measured, (8) children's age, (9) parents' age, (10) type of children's income (individual or family), (11) paper indicators, and (12) interaction of country and paper indicators.

Figure D.1
Trends of Inequality of Opportunity and Income Inequality, by Year: Australia, France, and United Kingdom

Panel A. Trends of inequality of opportunity and income inequality, by year: Australia (Leigh, 2007)

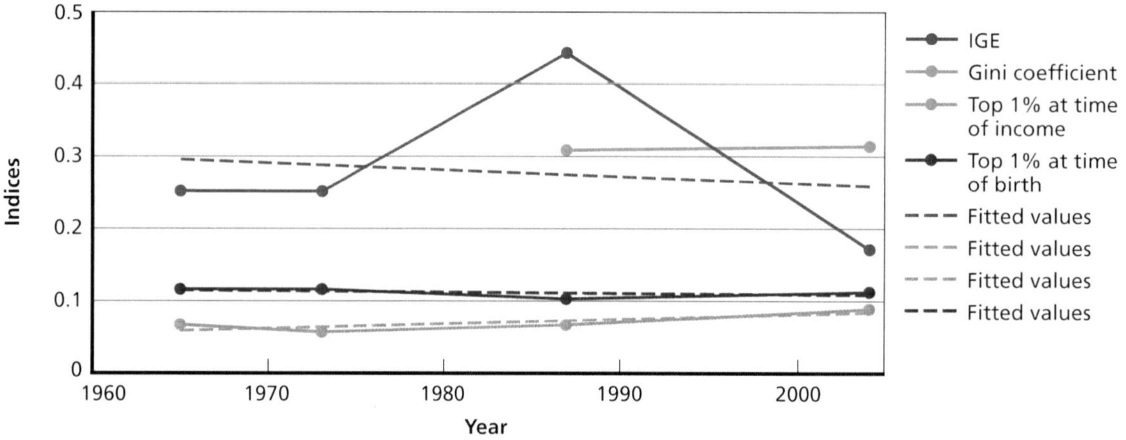

Panel B. Trends of inequality of opportunity and income inequality, by year: France (Lefranc and Trannoy, 2005)

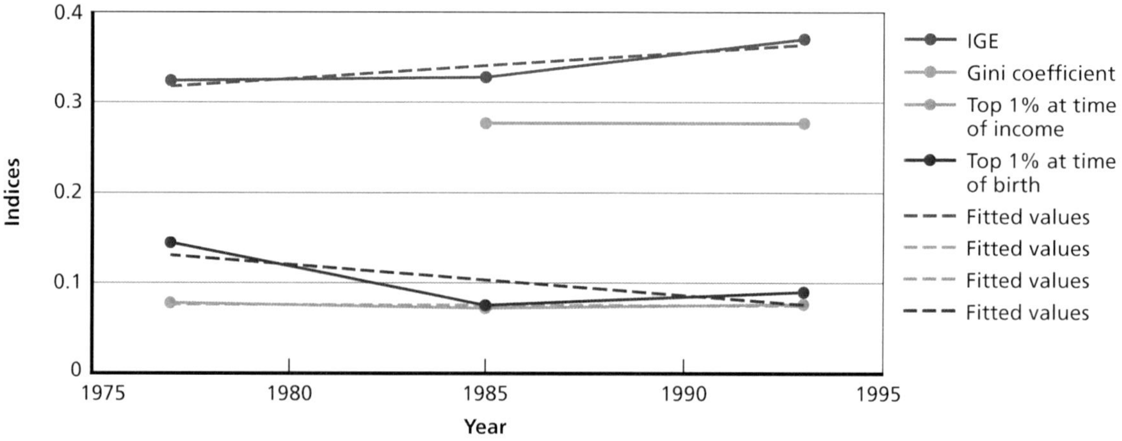

Panel C. Trends of inequality of opportunity and income inequality, by year: United Kingdom (Blanden and Machin, 2008)

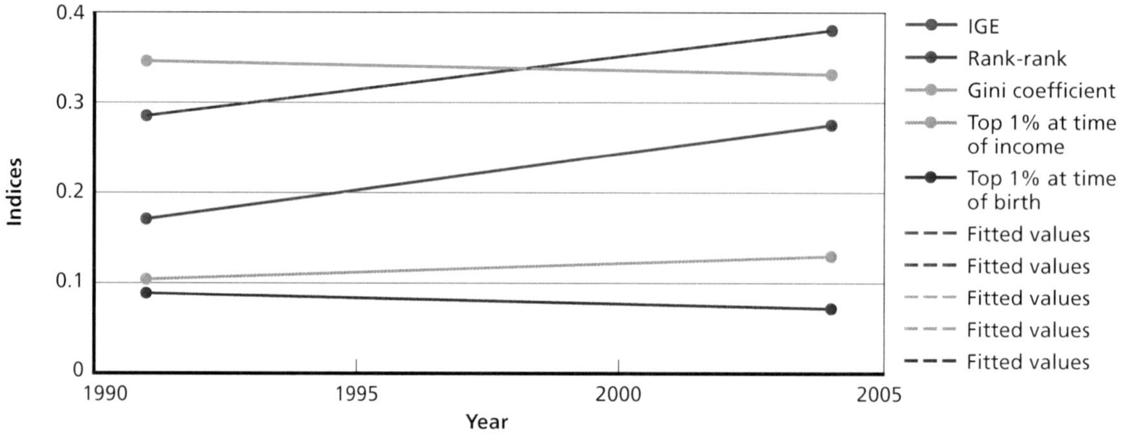

SOURCES: World Top Income Database, OECD.
RAND *RR1509-D.1*

References

Aaronson, Daniel, and Bhashkar Mazumder, "Intergenerational Economic Mobility in the US: 1940 to 2000," *Journal of Human Resources*, Vol. 43, No. 1, 2008, pp. 139–172.

Aizer, A., S. Eli, J. P. Ferrie, and A. Lleras-Muney, "The Long Term Impact of Cash Transfers to Poor Families," Working Paper No. 20103, Cambridge, Mass., National Bureau of Economic Research, 2014.

Almond, D., "Is the 1918 Influenza Pandemic Over? Long-Term Effects of in Utero Influenza Exposure in the Post-1940 U.S. Population," *Journal of Political Economy*, Vol. 114, No. 4, 2006, pp. 672–712.

Almond, D., and J. Currie, "Killing Me Softly: The Fetal Origins Hypothesis," *Journal of Economic Perspectives*, Vol. 25, No. 3, 2011, pp. 153–172.

Almond, D., H. Hoynes, and D. Schanzenbach, "Inside the War on Poverty: The Impact of Food Stamps on Birth Outcomes," *Review of Economics and Statistics*, Vol. 93, No. 2, 2011, pp. 387–403.

Alvaredo, Facundo, Anthony B. Atkinson, Thomas Piketty, and Emmanuel Saez, "The Top 1 Percent in International and Historical Perspective," *Journal of Economic Perspectives*, Vol. 27, No. 3, 2013, pp. 3–20.

Amaral, Ernesto, and Francisco Perez-Arce, "A Meta-Regression Analysis of Intergenerational Transmission of Income and the 'Great-Gatsby Curve'," unpublished manuscript, 2015.

Atkinson, A. B., *Inequality: What Can Be Done?* Cambridge, Mass.: Harvard University Press, 2015.

Atkinson, A. B., and Salvatore Morelli, *Chartbook of Economic Inequality*, March 8, 2014. As of March 1, 2015:
http://papers.ssrn.com/sol3/papers.cfm?abstract_id=2422269

Atkinson, A. B., T. Piketty, and E. Saez, "Top Incomes in the Long Run of History," *Journal of Economic Literature*, Vol. 49, No. 1, 2011, pp. 3–71.

Auten, G., and G. Gee, "Income Mobility in the United States: New Evidence from Income Tax Data," *National Tax Journal*, 2009, pp. 301–328.

Autor, D. H., F. Levy, and R. J. Murnane, "The Skill Content of Recent Technological Change: An Empirical Exploration," *Quarterly Journal of Economics*, Vol. 118, No. 4, 2003, pp. 1279–1333.

Autor, D. H., L. F. Katz, and M. S. Kearney, "The Polarization of the US Labor Market," *American Economic Review*, Vol. 96, No. 2, 2006, pp. 189–194.

———, "Trends in U.S. Wage Inequality: Revising the Revisionists," *Review of Economics and Statistics*, Vol. 90, No. 2, 2008, pp. 300–323.

Autor, David, David Dorn, and Gordon H. Hanson, "The China Syndrome: Local Labor Market Effects of Import Competition in the United States," *American Economic Review*, Vol. 103, No. 6, 2013, pp. 2121–2168.

Barnett, W. S., K. Jung, M. J. Youn, and E. C. Frede, "Abbott Preschool Program Longitudinal Effects Study: Fifth Grade Follow-Up," New Brunswick, N.J.: National Institute for Early Education Research, 2013.

Becker, G. S., "Investment in Human Capital: A Theoretical Analysis," *Journal of Political Economy*, Vol. 70, No. 5, 1962, pp. 9–49.

Becker, G. S., and N. Tomes, "An Equilibrium Theory of the Distribution of Income and Intergenerational Mobility," *Journal of Political Economy*, Vol. 87, No. 6, 1979, pp. 1153–1189.

Bhattacharya, J., J. Currie, and S. Haider, "Breakfast of Champions? The Nutritional Effects of the School Breakfast Program," *Journal of Human Resources*, Vol. 41, 2006, pp. 445–466.

Bitler, M. P., and L. A. Karoly, "Intended and Unintended Effects of the War on Poverty: What Research Tells Us and Implications for Policy," *Journal of Policy Analysis and Management*, Vol. 34, No. 3, 2015, pp. 639–696.

Björklund, A., and K. G. Salvanes, "Education and Family Background: Mechanisms and Policies," *Handbook of the Economics of Education*, Vol. 3, 2011, pp. 201–247.

Black, S. E., and P. J. Devereux, "Recent Developments in Intergenerational Mobility," in O. Ashenfelter and D. Card, eds., *Handbook of Labor Economics*, Vol. 4B, Amsterdam: Elsevier, 2011, pp. 1487–1541.

Black, S. E., P. J. Devereux, and K. G. Salvanes, "Why the Apple Doesn't Fall Far: Understanding Intergenerational Transmission of Human Capital," *American Economic Review*, Vol. 95, No. 1, 2005, pp. 437–449.

———, "From the Cradle to the Labor Market? The Effect of Birth Weight on Adult Outcomes," *Quarterly Journal of Economics*, Vol. 122, No. 1, 2007, pp. 409–439.

Blanden, J., P. Gregg, and L. Macmillan, "Accounting for Intergenerational Income Persistence: Noncognitive Skills, Ability and Education," *Economic Journal*, Vol. 117, No. 519, 2007, pp. C43–C60.

Blanden, B., and S. Machin, "Up and Down the Generational Income Ladder in Britain: Past Changes and Future Prospects," *National Institute Economic Review*, Vol. 205, No. 1, 2008, pp. 101–116.

Blau, D., "Child Care Subsidy Programs," in R. Moffitt, ed., *Means-Tested Transfer Programs in the United States*, Chicago: University of Chicago Press, 2003.

Blau, D., and E. Tekin, "The Determinants and Consequences of Child Care Subsidies for Single Mothers in the USA," *Journal of Population Economics*, Vol. 20, No. 4, 2007, pp. 719–741.

Borjas, G. J., R. B. Freeman, and L. F. Katz, "On the Labor Market Effects of Immigration and Trade," in George J. Borjas and Richard B. Freeman, eds., *Immigration and the Workforce: Economic Consequences for the United States and Source Areas*, Chicago: University of Chicago Press, 1992, pp. 213–244.

Bound, J., R. Burkhauser, and A. Nichols, "Tracking the Household Income of SSDI and SSI Applicants," in S. Polachek, ed., *Worker Well-Being and Public Policy, Research in Labor Economics*, Vol. 22. Amsterdam: Elsevier Science, 2003, pp. 113–159.

Bound, J., and G. E. Johnson, "Changes in the Structure of Wages During the 1980's: An Evaluation of Alternative Explanations," *American Economic Review*, Vol. 82, No. 3, 1992, pp. 371–392.

Bourguignon, F., and C. Morrisson, "Inequality Among World Citizens: 1820–1992," *American Economic Review*, Vol. 92, No. 4, 2002, pp. 727–744.

Brandolini, A., and G. Vecchi, "The Well-Being of Italians: A Comparative Historical Approach," Bank of Italy Economic History Working Paper No. 19, 2011.

Burkhauser, R. V., J. Larrimore, and K. I. Simon, "A 'Second Opinion' on the Economic Health of the American Middle Class," *National Tax Journal*, Vol. 65, No. 1, 2012, pp. 7–32.

Campbell, F. A., C. T. Ramey, E. Pungello, J. Sparling, and S. Miller-Johnson, "Early Childhood Education: Young Adult Outcomes from the Abecedarian Project," *Applied Developmental Science*, Vol. 6, No. 1, 2002, pp. 142–157.

Card, D., and J. E. DiNardo, "Skill-Biased Technological Change and Rising Wage Inequality: Some Problems and Puzzles," *Journal of Labor Economics*, Vol. 20, No. 4, 2002, pp. 733–783.

Carneiro, P., and J. J. Heckman, "The Evidence on Credit Constraints in Post-Secondary Schooling," *Economic Journal*, Vol. 112, No. 482, 2002, pp. 989–1018.

Carneiro, P., C. Meghir, and M. Parey, "Maternal Education, Home Environments, and the Development of Children and Adolescents," *Journal of the European Economic Association*, Vol. 11, No. 1, 2013, pp. 123–160.

Case, A., A. Fertig, and C. Paxson, "The Lasting Impact of Childhood Health and Circumstance," *Journal of Health Economics*, Vol. 24, No. 2, 2005, pp. 365–389.

Case, A., D. Lubotsky, and C. Paxson, "Economic Status and Health in Childhood: The Origins of the Gradient," *American Economic Review*, Vol. 92, No. 5, 2002, pp. 1308–1334.

Center for Economic and Policy Research, *March CPS Uniform Extracts*, Version 0.9.9.1, Washington, D.C., undated. As of March 1, 2015:
http://ceprdata.org/cps-uniform-data-extracts/march-cps-supplement/march-cps-data/

Chantrill, Christopher, ed., "US Entitlement Spending Growth," USgovernmentspending.com, website, undated. As of March 1, 2015:
http://www.usgovernmentspending.com/entitlement_spending

Chen, Wen-Hao, Michael Förster, and Ana Llena-Nozal "Demographic or Labour Market Trends: What Determines the Distribution of Household Earnings in OECD Countries?" *OECD Journal: Economic Studies*, Vol. 2013/1, 2014.

Chetty, R., N. Hendren, and L. F. Katz, *The Effects of Exposure to Better Neighborhoods on Children: New Evidence from the Moving to Opportunity Experiment*, National Bureau of Economic Research, 2015.

Chetty, R., N. Hendren, P. Kline, and E. Saez, "Where Is the Land of Opportunity? The Geography of Intergenerational Mobility in the United States," *Quarterly Journal of Economics*, Vol. 129, No. 4, 2014b, pp. 1553–1623.

Chetty, R., N. Hendren, P. Kline, E. Saez, and N. Turner, "Is the United States Still a Land of Opportunity? Recent Trends in Intergenerational Mobility," *American Economic Review*, Vol. 104, No. 5, 2014a, pp. 141–147.

Cohodes, S., D. Grossman, S. Kleiner, and M. Lovenheim, "The Effect of Child Health Insurance Access on Schooling: Evidence from Public Insurance Expansions," NBER Working Paper No. 20178, Cambridge, Mass.: National Bureau of Economic Research, 2014. As of March 1, 2015:
http://www.nber.org/papers/w20178

Corak, M., "Inequality from Generation to Generation: The United States in Comparison," in Robert Rycroft, ed., The Economics of Inequality, Poverty, and Discrimination in the 21st Century, Santa Barbara, Calif.: ABC-CLIO, 2013a.

———, "Income Inequality, Equality of Opportunity, and Intergenerational Mobility," *Journal of Economic Perspectives*, Vol. 27, No. 3, 2013b, pp. 79–102.

Corak, M., and P. Piraino, "The Intergenerational Transmission of Employers," *Journal of Labor Economics*, Vol. 29, No. 1, 2011 pp. 37–68.

Cunha, Flavio, and James Heckman, "The Technology of Skill Formation," *American Economic Review*, Vol. 97, No. 2, May 2007, pp. 31–47, online appendix. As of March 1, 2015:
http://jenni.uchicago.edu/tech-skill/webappendix.pdf

Currie, J., Decker, S. and Lin, W., "Has Public Health Insurance for Older Children Reduced Disparities in Access to Care and Health Outcomes?" *Journal of Health Economics*, Vol 27, No. 6, 2008, pp. 1567–1581.

Currie, Janet, and Ishita Rajani, "Within-Mother Estimates of the Effects of WIC on Birth Outcomes in New York City," *Economic Inquiry*, Vol. 53, No. 4, 2015, pp. 1691–1701.

Currie, J., and M. Stabile, "Socioeconomic Status and Child Health: Why Is the Relationship Stronger for Older Children?" *American Economic Review*, Vol. 93, No. 5, 2003, pp. 1813–1823.

Currie, J., M. Stabile, P. Manivong, and L. L. Roos, "Child Health and Young Adult Outcomes," *Journal of Human Resources*, Vol 45, No. 3, 2010, pp. 517–548.

Cutler, David M., and Lawrence F. Katz, "Rising Inequality? Changes in the Disbribution of Income and Consumption in the 1980s," *American Economic Association Papers and Proceedings*, Vol. 82, No. 2, May 1992.

Dahl, Gordon B., and Lance Lochner, "The Impact of Family Income on Child Achievement: Evidence from the Earned Income Tax Credit," *American Economic Review*, Vol. 102, No. 5, 2012, pp. 1927–1956.

Deaton, A., *The Great Escape: Health, Wealth, and the Origins of Inequality*, Princeton, N.J.: Princeton University Press, 2013.

Deming, D., "Early Childhood Intervention and Life-Cycle Skill Development: Evidence from Head Start," *American Economic Journal: Applied Economics*, Vol. 1, No. 3, 2009, pp. 111–134.

Dickert-Conlin, Stacy, and Scott Houser, "EITC and Marriage," *National Tax Journal*, Vol. 55, No. 1, March 2002, pp. 25–40.

DiNardo, J., N. M. Fortin, and T. Lemieux, "Labor Market Institutions and the Distribution of Wages, 1973–1992: A Semiparametric Approach," *Econometrica*, Vol. 64, No. 5, 1996, pp. 1001–1044.

Duggan, M., and M. Kearney, "The Impact of Child SSI Enrollment on Household Outcomes: Evidence from the SIPP," *Journal of Policy Analysis and Management*, Vol. 26, No. 4, 2007, pp. 861–886.

Duncan, G. J., P. A. Morris, and C. Rodrigues, "Does Money Really Matter? Estimating Impacts of Family Income on Young Children's Achievement with Data from Random-Assignment Experiments," *Developmental Psychology*, Vol. 47, No. 5, 2011, pp. 1263–1279.

Dustmann, C., J. Ludsteck, and U. Schonberg, "Revisiting the German Wage Structure," *Quarterly Journal of Economics*, Vol. 124, No. 2, 2009, pp. 843–881.

Dynarski, S., and J. Scott-Clayton, "Financial Aid Policy: Lessons from Research," *Future of Children*, Vol. 23, No. 1, 2013, pp. 67–91.

Eissa, N., and H. Hoynes, "Taxes and the Labor Market Participation of Married Couples: The Earned Income Tax Credit," *Journal of Public Economics*, Vol. 88, 2004, pp. 1931–1958.

Ellwood, David, "The Impact of the Earned Income Tax Credit and Social Policy Reforms on Work, Marriage, and Living Arrangements," *National Tax Journal*, Vol. 53, No. 4, Part 2, 2000, pp. 1063–1105.

Equality of Opportunity Project, "Previous Research: Is America the 'Land of Opportunity'?" website, Harvard University, undated. As of March 1, 2015:
http://www.equality-of-opportunity.org

Evans, W., and C. Garthwaite, "Giving Mom a Break: The Impact of Higher EITC Payments on Maternal Health," *American Economic Journal: Economic Policy*, Vol. 6, No. 2, 2014, pp. 258–290.

Fraker, T., A. Martini, and J. Ohls, "The Effect of Food Stamp Cash-out on Food Expenditures: An Assessment of the Findings from Four Demonstrations," *Journal of Human Resources*, Vol. 30, No. 4, 1995, pp. 633–649.

Friswold, David E., "Nutrition and Cognitive Achievement: An Evaluation of the School Breakfast Program," *Journal of Public Economics*, Vol. 124, 2015, pp. 91–104.

Garrett, B., and S. Glied, "Does State AFDC Generosity Affect Child SSI Participation?" *Journal of Policy Analysis and Management*, Vol. 19, No. 2, 2000, pp. 275–295.

Gelber, A., and A. Isen, "Children's Schooling and Parents' Behavior: Evidence from the Head Start Impact Study," *Journal of Public Economics*, Vol. 101, 2013, pp. 25–38.

Gennetian, L. A., and C. Miller, *Reforming Welfare and Rewarding Work: Final Report on the Minnesota Family Investment Program, Vol. 2, Effects on Children*, New York: Manpower Demonstration Research Corporation, 2000.

Gennetian, L. A., M. Sciandra, L. Sanbonmatsu, J. Ludwig, L. F. Katz, G. J. Duncan, J. R. Kling, and R. C. Kessler, "The Long-Term Effects of Moving to Opportunity on Youth Outcomes," *Cityscape: A Journal of Policy Development and Research*, Vol. 14 No. 2, 2012, 137–168.

Gertler, P., J. Heckman, R. Pinto, A. Zanolini, C. Vermeersch, S. Walker, S. M. Chang, and S. Grantham-McGregor, "Labor Market Returns to an Early Childhood Stimulation Intervention in Jamaica," *Science*, Vol. 344, No. 6187, 2014, pp. 998–1001.

Goldin, C., and S. R. Cellini, "Does Federal Student Aid Raise Tuition? New Evidence on For-Profit Colleges," *American Economic Journal: Economic Policy*, Vol. 6, 2014, pp. 174–206.

Goldin, C., and L. F. Katz, "The Legacy of U.S. Educational Leadership: Notes on Distribution and Economic Growth in the 20th Century," *American Economic Review*, Vol. 91, No. 2, 2001, pp. 18–23.

———, *The Race Between Education and Technology*, Cambridge, Mass.: Belknap Press, 2010.

Goos, M., and A. Manning, "Lousy and Lovely Jobs: The Rising Polarization of Work in Britain," *Review of Economics and Statistics*, Vol. 89, No. 1, 2007, pp. 118–133.

Goos, M., A. Manning, and A. Salomons, "Job Polarization in Europe," *American Economic Review*, Vol. 99, No. 2, 2009, pp. 58–63.

Hair, N. L., J. L. Hanson, B. L. Wolfe, and S. D. Pollak, "Association of Child Poverty, Brain Development, and Academic Achievement," *JAMA Pediatrics*, Vol. 169, No. 9, 2015, pp. 822–829.

Hamermesh, D. S., "The Timing of Work over Time," *Economic Journal*, Vol. 109, No. 452, 1999, pp. 37–66.

Hart, B., and T. R. Risley, "The Early Catastrophe: The 30 Million Word Gap by Age 3," *American Educator*, Vol. 27, No. 1, 2003, pp. 4–9.

Heckman, J. J., "The Economics, Technology, and Neuroscience of Human Capability Formation," *Proceedings of the National Academy of Sciences*, Vol. 104, No. 33, 2007, pp. 13250–13255.

Heckman, J. J., S. H. Moon, R. Pinto, P. A. Savelyev, and A. Yavitz, "The Rate of Return to the High/Scope Perry Preschool Program," *Journal of Public Economics*, Vol. 94, No. 1, 2010, pp. 114–128.

Herbst, C. M., and E. Tekin, "Child Care Subsidies, Maternal Health, and Child-Parent Interactions: Evidence from Three Nationally Representative Datasets," *Health Economics*, Vol. 23, No. 8, 2014, pp. 894–916.

Hertz, Tom, Tamara Jayasundera, Patrizio Piraino, Sibel Selcuk, Nicole Smith, and Alina Verashchagina, "The Inheritance of Educational Inequality: International Comparisons and Fifty-Year Trends," *B. E. Journal of Economic Analysis and Policy*, Vol. 7, No. 2, 2007, Article 10.

Hilger, N. G., *The Great Escape: Intergenerational Mobility Since 1940*, National Bureau of Economic Research Working Paper No. 21217, 2015.

Hill, C. J., W. T. Gormley, Jr., and S. Adelstein, "Do the Short-Term Effects of a Strong Preschool Program Persist?" Georgetown University, Center for Research on Children in the U.S. Working Paper 18, 2012. As of March 1, 2015:
https://georgetown.app.box.com/s/nhe5k1ji035bmblufu5o

Holzer, H. J., "Search Method Use by Unemployed Youth," *Journal of Labor Economics*, Vol. 6, No. 1, 1988, pp. 1–20.

Hotz, V. J., C. Mullin, and J. K. Scholz, "Examining the Effect of the Earned Income Tax Credit on the Labor Market Participation of Families on Welfare," NBER Working Paper No. 11968, Cambridge, Mass.: National Bureau of Economic Research, 2006. As of March 1, 2015:
http://www.nber.org/papers/w11968.pdf

Hoynes, H., and D. Schanzenbach, "Work Incentives and the Food Stamp Program," *Journal of Public Economics*, Vol. 96, 2012, pp. 151–162.

Hoynes, H., D. Miller, and D. Simon, "Income, the Earned Income Tax Credit, and Infant Health," *American Economic Journal: Economic Policy*, Vol. 7, No. 1, 2015, pp. 172–211.

Hoynes, H., M. Page, and A. H. Stevens, "Can Targeted Transfers Improve Birth Outcomes?: Evidence from the Introduction of the WIC Program," *Journal of Public Economics*, Vol. 95, No. 7, 2011, pp. 813–827.

Huston, A., C. Miller, L. Richburg-Hayes, G. J. Duncan, C. A. Eldred, T. S. Weisner, E. Lowe, V. C. McLoyd, D. A. Crosby, M. N. Ripke, and C. Redcross, *New Hope for Families and Children: Five-Year Results of a Program to Reduce Poverty and Reform Welfare*, New York: Urban Education, 2003.

Internal Revenue Service, "2015 EITC Income Limits, Maximum Credit Amounts and Tax Law Updates," web page, March 2014. As of March 1, 2015:
https://www.irs.gov/Credits-&-Deductions/Individuals/Earned-Income-Tax-Credit/EITC-Income-Limits-Maximum-Credit-Amounts

Joyce, T., A. Racine, and C. Yunzal-Butler, "Reassessing the WIC Effect: Evidence from the Pregnancy Nutrition Surveillance System," *Journal of Policy Analysis and Management*, Vol. 27, No. 2, 2008, pp. 277–303.

Juhn, C., K. M. Murphy, and B. Pierce, "Wage Inequality and the Rise in Returns to Skill," *Journal of Political Economy*, Vol. 101, No. 3, 1993, pp. 410–442.

Kahn, L. M., "Labor Market Policy: A Comparative View on the Costs and Benefits of Labor Market Flexibility," *Journal of Policy Analysis and Management*, Vol. 31, No. 1, 2012, pp. 94–110.

Kanbur, R., C. Rhee, and J. Zhuang, eds., *Inequality in Asia and the Pacific: Trends, Drivers, and Policy Implications*, London: Asian Development Bank and Routledge, 2014.

Karoly, L. A., "Changes in the Distribution of Individual Earnings in the United States: 1967–1986," *Review of Economics and Statistics*, Vol. 74, No. 1, 1992, pp. 107–115.

———, "Investing in the Future: Reducing Poverty Through Human Capital Investments," in S. H. Danziger and R. H. Haveman, eds., *Understanding Poverty*, New York: Russell Sage Foundation; Cambridge, Mass.: Harvard University Press, 2001, pp. 314–356, 507–552.

Karoly, Lynn A., and Gary Burtless, "Demographic Change, Rising Earnings Inequality, and the Distribution of Personal Well-Being, 1959–1989," *Demography*, Vol. 32, No. 3, 1995, pp. 379–405.

Katz, L. F., and K. M. Murphy, "Changes in Relative Wages, 1963–1987: Supply and Demand Factors," *Quarterly Journal of Economics*, Vol. 107, No. 1, 1992, pp. 35–78.

Kling, J. R., J. B. Liebman, and L. F. Katz, "Experimental Analysis of Neighborhood Effects," *Econometrica*, Vol. 75, No. 1, 2007, pp. 83–119.

Kling, J. R., J. Ludwig, and L. F. Katz, "Neighborhood Effects on Crime for Female and Male Youth: Evidence from a Randomized Housing Voucher Experiment," *Quarterly Journal of Economics*, Vol. 120, No. 1, 2005, pp. 87–130.

Krueger, A. B., "How Computers Have Changed the Wage Structure: Evidence from Microdata, 1984–1989," *Quarterly Journal of Economics*, Vol. 108, No. 1, 1993, pp. 33–60.

Krueger, Alan, chairman, Council of Economic Advisers, "The Rise and Consequences of Inequality in the United States," speech given at the Center for American Progress, January 12, 2012. As of September 4, 2014: https://www.whitehouse.gov/sites/default/files/krueger_cap_speech_final_remarks.pdf

Krugman, P. R., "Technology, Trade and Factor Prices," *Journal of International Economics*, Vol. 50, No. 1, 2000, pp. 51–71.

———, "Trade and Wages, Reconsidered," *Brookings Papers on Economic Activity*, Spring 2008, pp. 103–154.

Kubik, J., "Incentives for the Identification and Treatment of Children with Disabilities: The Supplemental Security Income Program," *Journal of Public Economics*, Vol. 73, 1999, pp. 187–215.

Kuznets, S., "Economic Growth and Income Inequality," *American Economic Review*, Vol. 45, No. 1, 1955, pp. 1–28.

Lakner, C., and B. Milanovic, *Global Income Distribution: From the Fall of the Berlin Wall to the Great Recession*, Policy Research Working Paper No. 6719, Washington, D.C., World Bank, 2013.

Lawrence, R. Z., M. J. Slaughter, R. E. Hall, S. J. Davis, and R. H. Topel, "International Trade and American Wages in the 1980s: Giant Sucking Sound or Small Hiccup?" *Brookings Papers on Economic Activity: Microeconomics 2*, 1993, pp. 161–226.

Lee, D. S., "Wage Inequality in the United States During the 1980s: Rising Dispersion or Falling Minimum Wage?" *Quarterly Journal of Economics*, Vol. 114, No. 3, 1999, pp. 977–1023.

Lefranc, A., and A. Trannoy, "Intergenerational Earnings Mobility in France: Is France More Mobile than the US?" *Annales d'Économie et de Statistique*, Vol. 78, 2005, pp. 57–77.

Leigh, A., "Intergenerational Mobility in Australia," *B. E. Journal of Economic Analysis and Policy*, Vol. 7, No. 2, 2007, Article 6.

Levine, P., and D. Schanzenbach, "The Impact of Children's Public Health Insurance Expansions on Educational Outcomes," *Frontiers in Health Policy Research*, Vol. 12, No. 1, 2009.

Lindert, P. H., and J. G. Williamson, *American Incomes 1774–1860*, National Bureau of Economic Research Working Paper No 18396, 2012.

López-Calva, L. F., and Nora Lustig, *Declining Inequality in Latin America: A Decade of Progress?* Washington, D.C.: Brookings Institution Press and UN Development Programme, 2010.

Loury, L. D., "Some Contacts Are More Equal Than Others: Informal Networks, Job Tenure, and Wages," *Journal of Labor Economics*, Vol. 24, No. 2, 2006, pp. 299–318.

Ludwig, J., G. J. Duncan, L. A. Gennetian, L. F. Katz, R. C. Kessler, J. R. Kling, and L. Sanbonmatsu, "Long-Term Neighborhood Effects on Low-Income Families: Evidence from Moving to Opportunity" *American Economic Review*, Vol. 103, No. 3, 2013, pp. 226–231.

Maddison Project, database, 2013 version. As of March 1, 2015:
www.ggdc.net/maddison/

Maurin, Eric, and Sandra McNally, "Vive la Révolution! Long-Term Educational Returns of 1968 to the Angry Students," *Journal of Labor Economics*, Vol. 26, No. 1, 2008, pp. 1–33.

Meyer, B., and D. Rosenbaum, "Welfare, the Earned Income Tax Credit, and the Labor Supply of Single Mothers," *Quarterly Journal of Economics*, Vol. 116, 2001, pp. 1063–1114.

Meyer, Bruce D., and James X. Sullivan, "Winning the War: Poverty form the Great Society to the Great Recession," *Brookings Papers on Economic Activity*, Fall 2012, pp. 133–200.

Milanovic, B., P. H. Lindert, and J. G. Williamson, *Measuring Ancient Inequality*, National Bureau of Economic Research Working Paper No. 13550, 2007.

Millenky, M., D. Bloom, S. Muller-Ravett, and J. Broadus, J., *Staying on Course: Three-Year Results of the National Guard Youth ChalleNGe Evaluation*, New York: Manpower Development Research Corporation, 2011.

Mincer, J., "Investment in Human Capital and Personal Income Distribution," *Journal of Political Economy*, Vol. 66, No. 4, 1958, pp. 281–302.

Mitchell, Josh, "Educational Attainment and Earnings Inequality Among US-Born Men: A Lifetime Perspective," Washington, D.C.: Urban Institute, April 2014. As of March 1, 2015:
http://www.urban.org/research/publication/educational-attainment-and-earnings-inequality-among-us-born-men/view/full_report

Mueller, H. M., P. P. Ouimet, and E. Simintzi, "Wage Inequality and Firm Growth," National Bureau of Economic Research w20876, 2015.

Murphy, K. M., and F. Welch, "The Structure of Wages," *Quarterly Journal of Economics*, Vol. 107, No. 1, 1992, pp. 285–326.

OECD—*See* Organisation for Economic Co-operation and Development.

Organisation for Economic Co-operation and Development, *Divided We Stand: Why Inequality Keeps Rising*, Paris: OECD Publishing, 2011. As of March 1, 2015:
http://dx.doi.org/10.1787/9789264119536-en

Oi, W. Y., and T. L. Idson, "Firm Size and Wages," in *Handbook of Labor Economics, Vol. 3, Part B*, Amsterdam: Elsevier, 1999, pp. 2165–2214.

Oreopoulos, P., "The Long-Run Consequences of Living in a Poor Neighborhood," *Quarterly Journal of Economics*, Vol. 118, No. 4, 2003 pp. 1533–1575.

Oreopoulos, P., M. E. Page, and A. H. Stevens, "The Intergenerational Effects of Compulsory Schooling," *Journal of Labor Economics*, Vol. 24, No. 4, 2006, pp. 729–760.

Philippon, T., and A. Reshef, "Wages and Human Capital in the US Finance Industry: 1909–2006," *Quarterly Journal of Economics*, Vol. 127, No. 4, 2012, pp. 1551–1609.

Pierce, B., "Compensation Inequality," *Quarterly Journal of Economics*, Vol. 116, No. 4, 2001, pp. 1493–1525.

Piketty, T., *Capital in the Twenty-First Century*, Cambridge, Mass.: Belknap Press of Harvard University Press, 2014.

Piketty, Thomas, and Emmanuel Saez, "The Evolution of Top Incomes: A Historical and International Perspective," National Bureau of Economic Research Working Paper No. 11955, 2006.

Piketty, Thomas, Emmanuel Saez, and Stefanie Stantcheva, "Optimal Taxation of Top Labor Incomes: A Tale of Three Elasticities," *American Economic Journal: Economic Policy*, Vol. 6, No. 1, 2014, pp. 230–271.

Piketty, T., and G. Zucman, "Wealth and Inheritance in the Long Run," in *Handbook of Income Distribution, Vol. 2B*, Amsterdam: Elsevier, 2015.

Prante, Gerald, and Scott A. Hodge, *The Distribution of Tax and Spending Policies in the United States*, Tax Foundation Special Report No. 211, November 8, 2013. As of July 31, 2015: http://taxfoundation.org/article/distribution-tax-and-spending-policies-united-states

Puma, M., S. Bell, R. Cook, and C. Heid, *Head Start Impact Study Final Report*, Washington, D.C.: U.S. Department of Health and Human Services, 2010.

Puma, M., S. Bell, R. Cook, C. Heid, P. Broene, F. Jenkins, A. Mashburn, and J. Downer, *Third Grade Follow-up to the Head Start Impact Study Final Report*, Office of Planning, Research and Evaluation Report 2012-45, Washington, D.C.: U.S. Department of Health and Human Services, 2012.

Restuccia, D., and C. Urrutia, "Intergenerational Persistence of Earnings: The Role of Early and College Education," *American Economic Review*, Vol. 94, No. 5, 2004, pp. 1354–1378.

Reynolds, A. J., J. A. Temple, S. R. Ou, I. A. Arteaga, and B. A. White, "School-Based Early Childhood Education and Age-28 Well-Being: Effects by Timing, Dosage, and Subgroups," *Science*, Vol. 333, No. 6040, 2011, pp. 360–364.

Roemer, J., R. Aaberge, U. Colombino, J. Fritzell, S. P. Jenkins, and A. Lefranc, "To What Extent Do Fiscal Regimes Equalize Opportunities for Income Acquisition Among Citizens?" *Journal of Public Economics*, Vol. 87, Nos. 3–4, 2003, pp. 539–565.

Sacerdote, B., "Nature and Nurture Effects on Children's Outcomes: What Have We Learned from Studies of Twins and Adoptees," *Handbook of Social Economics, Vol. 1*, Amsterdam: Elsevier, 2010, pp. 1–30.

Saez, E., and G. Zucman, "Wealth Inequality in the United States Since 1913: Evidence from Capitalized Income Tax Data," National Bureau of Economic Research Working Paper 20625, 2014.

Sanbonmatsu, L., J. R. Kling, G. J. Duncan, and J. Brooks-Gunn, "Neighborhoods and Academic Achievement Results from the Moving to Opportunity Experiment," *Journal of Human Resources*, Vol. 41, No. 4, 2006, pp. 649–691.

Schochet, P., J. Burghardt, and S. Glazerman, *National Job Corps Study: The Impacts of Job Corps on Participants' Employment and Related Outcomes*, Princeton, N.J.: Mathematica Policy Research, 2001.

Smith, J. P., and G. C. Smith, "Long-Term Economic Costs of Psychological Problems During Childhood," *Social Science and Medicine*, Vol. 71, No. 1, 2010, pp. 110–115.

Sobel, J., "Can We Trust Social Capital?" *Journal of Economic Literature*, Vol. 40, No. 1, 2002, pp. 139–154.

Spitz-Oener, A., "Technical Change, Job Tasks, and Rising Educational Demands: Looking Outside the Wage Structure," *Journal of Labor Economics*, Vol. 24, No. 2, 2006, pp. 235–270.

Strully, K., D. Rehkopf, and Z. Xuan, "The Effects of Prenatal Poverty on Infant Health: State Earned Income Tax Credits and Birth Weight," *American Sociological Review*, Vol. 75, No. 4, 2010, pp. 534–562.

Strumpf, E., "Medicaid's Effect on Single Women's Labor Supply: Evidence from the Introduction of Medicaid," *Journal of Health Economics*, Vol. 30, No. 3, 2011, pp. 531–548.

U.S. Census Bureau, *Income and Poverty in the United States: 2013*, Report No. P60-249, Washington, D.C., U.S. Department of Commerce, September 16, 2014.

van Zanden, J. L., J. Baten, M. Mira d'Ercole, A. Rijpma, C. Smith, and M. Timmer, eds., *How Was Life? Global Well-Being Since 1820*, Paris: OECD Publishing, 2014. As of July 31, 2015: http://adapt.it/englishbulletin/wp/wp-content/uploads/2014/10/oecd_2_10_2014.pdf

Vogel, Cheri A., Yange Xue, Emily M. Moiduddin, Ellen Eliason Kisker, and Barbara Lepidus Carlson, *Early Head Start Children in Grade 5: Long-Term Follow-Up of the Early Head Start Research and Evaluation Project Study Sample*, OPRE Report No. 2011-8. Washington, D.C.: U.S. Department of Health and Human Services, December 2010.

Walker, Susan P., Theodore D. Wachs, Sally Grantham-McGregor, Maureen M. Black, Charles A. Nelson, Sandra L. Huffman, Helen Baker-Henningham, Susan M. Chang, Jena D. Hamadani, Betsy Lozoff, Julie M. Meeks Gardner, Christine A. Powell, Atif Rahman, and Linda Richter, "Inequality in Early Childhood: Risk and Protective Factors for Early Child Development," *The Lancet*, Vol. 378, No. 9799, 2011 pp. 1325–1338.

Wolff, E. N., and M. Gittleman, "Inheritances and the Distribution of Wealth or Whatever Happened to the Great Inheritance Boom?" *Journal of Economic Inequality*, Vol. 12, No. 4, 2014, pp. 439–468.